CW01066937

MICROS AND MODEMS:
Telecommunicating with Personal Computers

Jack M. Nilles
Center for Futures Research
University of Southern California

CONTENTS

PREFACE

This book is an introduction to the rapidly growing field of computer communications. Its emphasis is on communication between microcomputers and other computers: micros, minis and mainframes. Written for the novice to computer communications, this book is intended to be a practical guide to developing a telecommunications capability for one's own personal computer, as well as communications software.

My reason for writing *Micros and Modems* is that the impact of telecommunicating personal computers on our future lives is likely to be significant— in the home as well as in the office. Yet most of the books on computer telecommunications present a severe case of overkill for the individual who is new to the game. The typical new owner of a microcomputer is not likely to want to dig through all the gory details of developing X.25 protocols and converting them to practice; he or she simply wants to get the thing to communicate somehow. And salespeople in computer stores are not always of infinite help in this regard. The user needs some continuing guidance—first to help select the necessary telecommunications hardware (in the most likely case that it isn't built into the computer), and then to develop or acquire the necessary software to get the hardware to function properly for the purpose the user had in mind. Once that capability is functioning, the computer owner will find a whole new area for useful and/or fun-filled telecommunications. With the present rate of development of telecommunications-based computer services, this field can only increase in variety and interest in the coming years.

You need not be an expert on computers or telecommunications or software to use this book successfully. You should know some of the basic jargon of the computer world, although all the computer-particular terms used are defined at least once. The first part of the book requires no technical knowledge whatsoever; its intent is to explain why you might be interested in telecommunicating with your computer, in case you aren't already.

The technical material starts in the second part of the book. It begins with an introduction to the hardware required for simple, direct computer-to-computer telecommunications, and then it goes on to telecommunications with modems over the telephone system. This latter topic occupies much of the rest of the book. The hardware descriptions are followed by chapters on developing your own telecommunications software. In order to understand the software chapters completely, you should have some knowledge of BASIC. However, if you are not a BASIC programmer, or any other kind of programmer, these chapters will still be helpful in explaining the procedures that telecommunications software must include.

After the software design issues are presented, we turn to one of the areas of extremely active development in computer communications: local area networks. This topic is likely to be of growing interest to managers and professionals who are concerned with, or involved in, office automation. The details of the design of local area networks are beyond the scope of this book; however, there is enough material included here to give the reader a feeling for the relative merits of different concepts of network design.

The final chapter deals with a few of the possible future applications of telecommunicating computers. The growing range of network information services, office automation, community bulletin boards, and telecommuting to work or to school are included, in the hopes that some of these topics may inspire you to invent your own applications.

As the personal computer market expands, a number of different telecommunications hardware and software packages are being sold. Some have extensive options; others are relatively limited. Even if you are going to buy only one of the packages and never to fiddle with it, I hope this book will provide you with a sound basis for making that selection. If you do want to try out some of your own communication ideas, I hope this will give you a sound basis for expansion.

In my books and other publications over the past decade or so, I have concentrated on the effects of computer and telecommunications technologies on society and on individuals. I have an abiding interest in these effects and am actively engaged in continuing my research in this regard. I am always interested in hearing about new applications of computers and telecommunications and about the results of those applications. Those interested in commenting upon these effects should write me in care of The Center for Futures Research, Graduate School of Business Administration, University of Southern California.

I would like to thank the many vendors of telecommunications equipment and software who provided background material for several portions of the book. Thanks are due also to Meryl Thomas, of Reston Publishing Company, for her expert supervision of the final preparation process. Most particularly, I thank my wife, Laila, for her encouragement, support, product testing, and good humor during the production process. This book was written entirely on a microcomputer system that has never failed me in the past four years, including the production of many reports and two books, thanks to Cromemco.

JACK M. NILLES
Los Angeles

INTRODUCTION

Microcomputers are the heroes of this book. Springing into the world in 1975 as the children of microelectronic and computer technologies, they have already titillated the imaginations, if not changed the lives, of people all over the world. In just a few years a new industry has sprouted. This industry had over a billion dollars of economic activity in 1981. More important, microcomputers will affect the lives of millions of people over the next few decades.

Telecommunications technologies also are the heroes of this book. Born before the turn of this century, telecommunications technology has become pervasive in most of the world. In the remotest deserts or deepest jungles one can find transistor radios. The influence of telecommunications on our daily lives and on world affairs is profound and immeasurable. Radio, television, and (perhaps most) the telephone are vital to us in our daily lives. Almost every facet of our existence is touched by telecommunications technology.

Most of us take telecommunications technology for granted. It is so much a part of our lives that we do not pay particular attention to it until it suddenly fails to provide the services to which we have become accustomed. Microcomputers are so new that they have not become comfortably familiar for most of us. But they are likely to do so in the not-too-distant future. Hundreds of thousands of people had purchased microcomputers by the end of 1980. Tens of millions will have bought them by the end of the century. A goodly portion of those people will not be content to use their computers in isolation from others. They will want to be able to communicate with each other.

This book has two purposes. First, it tells you *why* you might want a telecommunicating microcomputer, now or in the future. Second, it tells you *how* to do it: how to get a microcomputer to "talk" to another machine or to communicate directly with you. You are assumed to be inexpert at the intricacies of computer and telecommunications technologies but curious and mentally agile enough to be able to derive a sense of satisfaction from putting some components together and making them work properly. To put it another way, you do not even have to be spectacular at math, although it helps to be able to count.

This book is divided into two parts. The first part deals with the *why* of telecommunicating microcomputers. If you do not want to know why you may be doing this, skip to the second part. If you think you already know why, you also might skip to the second part; possibly you'll sneak back later for a look at the philosophy.

The second part deals with the *how* of microcomputer telecommunications. In some cases you can just hook a few components into your microcomputer,

The Future of Telecommunicating Small Computers

install the proper software, and communicate away; this part tells you about the available options. In other cases you may want to develop some capabilities customized to your particular needs. This is a common urge among even the lightly addicted computer enthusiasts. The tools and procedures you will need for this are also described in the second part.

First, however, let's discuss the reasons why telecommunicating small computers will be an important part of the future.

THE INFORMATION SOCIETY

When the United States officially became an independent nation in 1783 most of its inhabitants were farmers. The country remained mostly agricultural until late in the nineteenth century. Then, as a result of the industrial revolution, manufacturing became the dominant occupation and remained so until the mid-1950s. More workers were directly employed in operating lathes, assembling cars, and running drill presses than in any other sort of tasks.

The change began slowly, as most changes do, early in this century. Almost imperceptibly at first, then with accelerating momentum, more and more of us spent the major portions of our working lives dealing with information instead of farming or manufacturing or chopping trees or fighting fires. By the mid-1950s, as many of the U.S. population were employed in information work as were in manufacturing jobs. Today the majority of our national labor force does information work. We are an information society.

This preoccupation with information is not confined to our jobs. Our leisure time is also filled with information activities. Reading; watching TV; listening to the radio or the stereo; playing card, board, or computer games; and, of course, using your personal computer: all are information pursuits. The manipulation of information consumes far more of the waking, not to mention dreaming, hours of most of us than anything else.

Think about it for a while. What are information jobs? Surely writing is one. Teaching, bank clerking, acting, secretarying, selling, theorizing, drawing, and preaching are others. Those just named account for a goodly number of our citizens. But how about some of the non-information jobs mentioned earlier? Take farming. Modern farming technology includes many information functions. The use of soil-moisture, mineral-content, and crop-yield histories, as well as long-term weather forecasts, commodity-market trends, government price-support policies, and other information aids, is all part of the daily routine on an

3

increasing percentage of our farms. Farming just is not all plowing, planting, milking, and harvesting anymore. Farmers have become sophisticated information workers. The same can be said about many other formerly non-information occupations.

Information technologies are responsible for much of this change over the past two-score years; the telecommunication and computer technologies are the foremost among these change-makers. These two technologies develop considerable synergy (mutual positive feedback), the effects of which are just beginning to be seen in our daily lives. They act to intensify the information activity in our society; that is why it is important that we have some understanding of the ways these technologies can affect us and can work for us.

TELECOMMUNICATIONS GROWTH

The term "telecommunications" simply means communicating by electrical or electronic means. It covers a wide variety of methods of communications.

The Beginnings of Telecommunication

The first widespread telecommunications technology was the telegraph. The telegraph played an important role in the development of the United States and in the western movie. It enabled the rapid development of commerce by providing the ability to communicate changes in business conditions quickly between places far apart. The telegraph closely followed the railroad as the harbinger of twentieth-century society in the diminishing wilderness. The importance of the telegraph was underscored by the elaborate means taken to disrupt its service at times of tension, such as during the Civil War and in the bank robberies depicted in hundreds of westerns ground out over the past few decades. By the middle of the nineteenth century, the telegraph had clearly become a vital link in the daily activities of many parts of the nation.

A Technical Digression: Besides being the first major telecommunication technology, the telegraph was the first digital telecommunication technology. That is, the telegraph responds only to digital signals, simple *on* and *off* commands. Figure 1-1 shows a simple telegraph arrangement. The sending

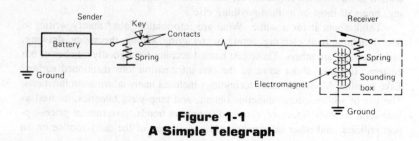

Figure 1-1
A Simple Telegraph

end of the system consists of a battery and a telegraph key. One side of the battery is connected to ground. (This is literally the case: the wire from, say, the negative side of the battery is connected to a conducting rod that is driven into the ground. The ground, that is, the upper surface of the earth, becomes the return conductor in the telegraph circuit; hence the term "ground," which is commonly used in electronics to denote the common signal-return conductor.) The other side of the battery is connected to one post of the telegraph key. The telegraph key is simply a switch. A small spring keeps it "open," that is, keeps the electrical circuit from being completed. When the telegraph operator presses down on the key, overcoming the pressure of the spring, the switch is closed and the circuit is completed. The resulting "signal," the change in the voltage on the telegraph wire from zero to whatever is the battery voltage (50 volts, for example), travels down the wire to the receiver at nearly the speed of light.

The receiver consists of two parts: an electromagnet inside a box (or on the side of some other form of sounding board), and a hinged, spring-loaded arm which resembles the telegraph key but is not part of the electrical circuit. The end of the arm opposite its hinged end has a small magnet or a piece of iron on it. This end is positioned opposite the electromagnet on the other side of the sounding board. When the signal comes in from the sender to the electromagnet, the electromagnet is activated and produces an instantaneous magnetic field. The piece of iron on the arm is attracted by the magnetic field, overcoming the force of the spring. The arm travels down toward the electromagnet and hits the sounding box with a resounding TOK. That is all there is to it.

The telegraph operator at the receiving end listens to the pattern of TOKs coming from the sounding box and mentally translates it into a sequence of letters and numbers. Two types of signals are sent: a single impulse, caused by the sender depressing and quickly releasing the key (a dot); and a rapid series of clicks or a buzz, depending on the particular details of the design of the telegraph system (a dash). Samuel Morse, the inventor of the telegraph, also invented a coding system for making the conversions between the clicks or buzzes and English letters, numbers, and punctuation marks: the Morse Code. In Figure 1-2 a sequence of dots and dashes spelling out SOS is depicted. The short pulses are dots, the longer pulses (about three times as long as the dots)

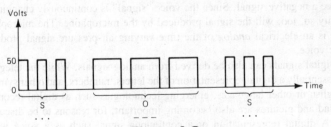

Figure 1-2
Morse Code: Digital Signals

are dashes. In contemporary electronic terms this mode of communication is called pulse-width modulation. In any case telegraph transmissions are digital communications; they use signals that are either *on* or *off*—nothing in between is considered.

The Rise of the Telephone

Although the telegraph is an excellent means of transmitting information that is somehow to be converted into writing, it lacks many features desirable for direct communication between human beings. Humans are not normally brought up to converse in dots and dashes. More compact language structures are usually used. The invention of the telephone was the next major step in the growing use of telecommunications. It brought immediate, natural, personal communications access, and eliminated need for learning complicated and unwieldy coding systems. The telephone quickly surpassed the telegraph for interpersonal messages that did not require written records. The growth in the number of telephones in use in the United States is shown in Figure 1-3.

Although the telegraph was the first great innovation in electronic communications, the telephone has been by far the most pervasive. Few homes in the United States today are without telephones. By telephone, you can communicate with almost any point on the face of the earth in a fraction of a second. As Figure 1-3 shows, there are two telephones in service today for every three people in the United States. As electronic technologies have improved so, too, have the quality, quantity, and reliability of telephone services, much as you may complain about them. As more and more computers become connected to the telephone lines the variety of communications options will become staggering.

A Technical Digression: Telephones communicate with each other using analog signals, as shown in Figure 1-4. The instantaneous intensity of a voice speaking into the telephone is converted to an instantaneous voltage by the telephone transmitter in the handset. For example, if the instantaneous voice-induced pressure on the microphone in the handset is positive (greater than the ambient air pressure), then the microphone will produce a positive signal. If the instantaneous pressure on the microphone is negative, then the microphone will produce a negative signal. Since the voice "signal" is continuously changing in intensity so, too, will the signal produced by the microphone. The microphone signal is an electrical *analog* of the time-varying air-pressure signal produced by the voice.

Digital signals can also be derived from analog signals. While the telegraph uses essentially a digital representation of the letters, numbers, and other symbols of English or other languages, emerging technologies such as digital recording of sound and pictures are also becoming important, for reasons to be discussed later. A digital representation of a continuous signal such as a voice would consist of a string of binary digits ("bits") representing the intensities of the signal at different instants of time. Figure 1-5 illustrates the concept. A digital communications system, instead of sending a continuously varying signal, would

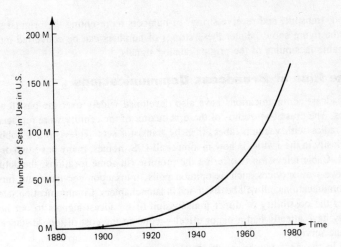

Figure 1-3
Growth in Telephone Installations

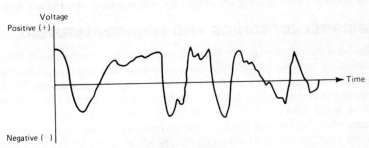

Figure 1-4
An Analog Signal

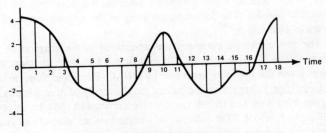

Figure 1-5
Deriving a Digital Signal

send, transmit, and receive strings of numbers representing the original signal, as the figure shows. Later these strings of numbers can be converted into reasonable facsimiles of the original analog signals.

The Rise of Broadcast Communications

Broadcast communications have also developed widely over the past few decades. The crystal-set radios of the first quarter of the century were replaced first by radios with vacuum tubes, then by transistor sets. Television, a hobbyist's curiosity in the 1940s, is now in almost all U.S. homes; many have two or more sets. Cable television is offering the promise (in some locations, the actuality) of two-way services such as opinion polls, transaction services, and message communications; all will be discussed in later chapters. Communication satellites offer the possibility of direct transmission of broadcast signals to our homes. They have already had a major effect—reducing the cost of long-distance telephone service.

In the next few years these telecommunications systems will undergo a major new transformation in technology, or a reversion to the original techniques, depending on how you look at it. Telephone systems will become all digital. Even voice transmission will become digital. Digital electronics will dominate the world of two-way communications, but that is getting ahead of our story.

MICROELECTRONICS AND MICROCOMPUTERS

The other critical chain of developments paralleling the growth of telecommunications has been the growth of electronics technologies. Electronics, particularly microelectronics, has an even shorter history than telecommunications. The microelectronics industry also has one of the highest rates of growth of any industry in the world. Carl Sagan, in his book *The Dragons of Eden*, noted that, if the entire fifteen-billion-year history of the universe were to be compressed into a single year, the recorded history of humanity would occupy the last ten seconds of December 31st; the history of the evolution of the general-purpose computer started three-tenths of a second before midnight; the history of the electronic computer and that of the microprocessor covers the last eight one-hundredths and the last eleven one-thousandths of the second before New Year's, respectively. In this relative instant, immense potential has developed for change in our earthly pursuits. The following are some of the major events in the development of electronics.

The first electronic computer was assembled in the years 1940–1942 by Professor John V. Atanasoff and Clifford Berry, a student, at Iowa State University. It was followed four years later by ENIAC (Electronic Numeral Integrator and Calculator), a huge machine built at the University of Pennsylvania. ENIAC weighed thirty tons, had 18,000 vacuum tubes, consumed 140 kilowatts of power, could perform about 5000 additions or subtractions per second and could store twenty 10-digit numbers in its memory! It was nonetheless a considerable advance over earlier mechanical computers that used gears or telegraph-like relays to act as computing elements.

The product that started the major and continuing surge in the development of computers was the transistor, invented by a team of scientists from Bell Telephone Laboratories in 1948. The transistor's relatively low power consumption and small size made it a natural candidate for the component-hungry computer. Using the transistor, the first commercial electronic computer was introduced by Univac in 1950. Fifty UNIVAC Is were built.

Computers depend critically on the number of memory cells and other computational elements they can access at any given moment. Thus, in general, the more memory and computational elements a computer has at its command, the more powerful it is and the more things it can do. In practice, things are often not quite so straightforward as this, but the general rule still holds for a given "generation" of computers. The pea-sized transistor occupied one one-hundredth the space of a vacuum tube and consumed proportionally less power, so transistorized computers had the basic potential of being in the order of 100 times as powerful as the earlier vacuum-tube machines. These general relationships still hold.

In 1959 the first integrated circuit was developed. This development constituted another great step forward in electronic technology. The integrated circuit contains a number of transistors, often together with other necessary electronic components such as resistors and capacitors. As time progressed the ability of the semiconductor manufacturers to cram more and more components on a single "chip" of silicon has steadily grown. In 1965 Dr. Gordon Moore announced his "law" that the complexity of a chip would double every year for ten years. It did. A typical state-of-the-art chip in 1975 had about 1000 times the complexity of an advanced chip of 1965.

One of the key fruits of this increasing complexity has been the microprocessor. The microprocessor is the brains of the microcomputer. The first microprocessor was produced in 1970 by Intel. It was a 4-bit chip (meaning that it processed data 4 bits, i.e., binary digits, at a time) similar to those routinely used now in most pocket calculators. The 4-bit microprocessor is what made the pocket calculator possible. It began the flood of smart devices which is still growing and which will continue to grow into the foreseeable future.

In 1970 there were slightly more than 100,000 computers of all kinds in existence in the world, most of them large machines requiring extensive support facilities, air-conditioned environments, and crews of maintenance technicians. In 1974 the first "personal" computer was sold, based on an 8-bit microprocessor, the Intel 8008. By the end of 1980 there were probably about 500,000 personal computers in existence—more than five times the number of computers of all sorts that were available a decade earlier. (In 1983, we're close to the three million mark.) The least expensive of today's personal computers, and many pocket calculators, can perform better than ENIAC.

The term "computer" is misleading, although it sticks with us for historical reasons. Microcomputers don't just compute, or calculate; they process symbols. The symbols can be related to anything: numbers, letters of the alphabet, musical notes, colors, whatever the machine's programmer desires. We live in a world of symbols. We communicate with symbols—sounds, signs, and sketches. Computers are increasingly becoming intermediaries in that communication. Microcomputers are expanding the diversity of those communications, and will continue to do so at least to the turn of the century.

ROBOTS AND AUTOMATION

Another product of these advancing technologies was once confined to the pages of science fiction magazines—robots and automation. Automation, of course, has been with us since before the beginning of the industrial revolution. The Jacquard looms run by punched cards began a trend in the nineteenth century that is now associated with the more recent technology of computers. In the middle of the twentieth century computer-like machine tools were perfected. Typically these tools were controlled by punched or magnetic tapes. The tapes contained the information necessary to drive the elements of the tool, such as a lathe, drill press, or milling machine, so that it would automatically and repetitively carve out the desired parts from raw metal. These techniques are still current in many of our factories engaged in mass production.

As computer technology became more sophisticated, and particularly as computers started to shrink, computers began to be used as more sophisticated controllers of the machine tools. The technology spread to other areas, such as the handling of hazardous materials and the performance of biochemical analyses for medical purposes. Automation started to be seen in many places other than the assembly line.

As the machine tool and other automated device technologies took advantage of the smaller, less expensive minicomputers, they began to become extremely sophisticated as compared to their fellows of the early '50s and '60s. Industrial robots appeared, first one or two at a time, then in sizeable quantities. Interestingly, although the term "robot" is commonly associated with the United States (despite its having been coined by a Czech), the majority of the recent developments and applications of industrial robots have occurred in Japan.

There are two reasons for the evolution of robots. First, automation technology in general has been proven in many applications to result in significant increases in industrial productivity. Robots allow automation to be extended to very complex industrial operations. Second, computer technology in general, and microelectronics in particular, are allowing these complex operations to be performed at cost and quality levels significantly better, in some cases, than the same operations performed by humans.

Most automated devices and machines operate in a "stand-alone" mode at present. That is, they, and their associated computers, are loaded with fixed programs that they proceed to follow without outside intervention. The machines change their operating patterns only if new programs are loaded into them, as may be done by changing their magnetic tapes. That is, they do not usually telecommunicate with other machines or with people in other locations. That "traditional" form of automation is now changing, because of the growing economies of microelectronics.

It is now feasible for industrial designers to conceive of general-purpose robots that have communication capability. Such robots can be programmed to make one type of part for a certain period and then switch to the manufacture of an entirely different type of part under the control, via telecommunications, of a remote operator or remote computer. The term "programmable automation" has been coined to describe this concept. The concept can be extended to the entire production process itself. Not only the activities of individual robots in the manufacturing process but the routing of parts and raw materials too can be under the control of a central computer system. The flow of parts may follow one pattern for a certain length of time, then switch to another pattern in tune with the changing of the programs in the production robots. The consequence of this is that in the fairly near future it will be possible to automate "job shop" operations—manufacturing processes that produce only a few, rather than millions of, identical parts.

Another important implication of this trend is that automated processes will start to appear in a number of very familiar places in the home and office as well as in the factory. Some simple forms of automation are quite familiar to most Americans: the washing machine and dryer. A common example of programmable automation in the home is the newer form of microwave oven and the video tape recorder. Home security systems are examples of automation in which the product is information, rather than some finished piece of goods. Automated house-cleaning systems may be just over the horizon for the "electronic cottage." Although, as in the factory, most of these home-based forms of automation operate in a stand-alone mode at present, it seems probable that the demand will increase in future years for wiring some or all of these together with a telecommunicating microcomputer. You might then think seriously of calling up your house (that is, phoning your home computer) and telling it to postpone dinner for a few minutes, check to see whether the lawn needs watering (and act accordingly), turn the lights on in the bedroom, and change the message in your phone answering machine—all of these tasks being performed by separate automated devices linked to your home microcomputer. Home is the robot, home from the sea, where once it was a pile of sand (silicon dioxide).

2

In the 1950s an individual would not have considered owning a computer for personal use. After all, a computer in those days cost millions of dollars. Now, thirty years later, a microprocessor with greater capability than ENIAC costs less than a set of movie tickets for a typical American family. Moore's Law, referred to earlier, can be stated another way: the power of a single state-of-the-art chip has been increasing by a factor of ten every three or four years. The cost of a given level of computer capability has been decreasing at a somewhat slower rate, because it costs more to make more complicated chips. Moore's second version of his law stretches that time out to about seven years—through the later '80s—for both the power and cost of microelectronics. Like most "laws" of this sort, Moore's is not a statement of demonstrable physical reality but a forecast of the continuing trend of development in the international microelectronics industry.

What this means in practical terms to the consumer of microelectronics hardware is that the choices available with even a modest investment will continue to expand at about an 18% to 39% annual rate, exclusive of the effects of inflation (and some other, non-technological factors covered in an earlier book). If a particular capability is not available this year at a price you can afford, stick around; it is likely that it will be available at an affordable price in the not-too-distant future. The dilemma facing the potential computer buyer is whether to buy today's machine, with incomplete capabilities, or to wait until the ideal machine arrives at some (still uncertain) point in the future.

Other issues also arise in this decision about when to buy or to upgrade computer capability, and how it should be done. For example, there is no single standard for the design and construction of a computer. The result is that there is a variety of microcomputers on the market today that are far from interchangeable at the hardware or even at the software level. This fact is not necessarily a problem if the microcomputer you own is relatively self-sufficient and does not require data, or access to programs, from machines of other types or manufacture. However, as you have now reached this point in the book, the chances are that you have discovered that you do now or will soon need access to other machines, one way or another, in your uses of microcomputers. As it turns out, *the use of telecommunications can often be a practical means for alleviating inter-computer compatibility problems.*

Of course, your problem may not be one of incompatibility at all. You may simply need to receive information or transmit it, for any of a variety of reasons.

Microcomputer Technology

Some possibilities are discussed in later chapters. In either case you will need one or more microcomputers and some form of telecommunications to effect the information transfer. In order to be able to examine the possible options, it is advisable first to review the basic makeup of the chief elements in these systems: the microcomputers themselves, and the telecommunications systems to which they may become attached. This and the following chapter provide the review. For details about specific systems the reader is advised to consult the manufacturer and/or a reputable dealer in the particular system of interest.

STAND-ALONE MICROCOMPUTERS

A typical stand-alone microcomputer system is shown in Figure 2-1. It consists of seven main physical components:

1. The *Central Processor Unit (CPU)*, using one or more microprocessors

2. The *main memory*, consisting of one or more *random-access memory (RAM)* units, and possibly some *read-only memory (ROM)* units

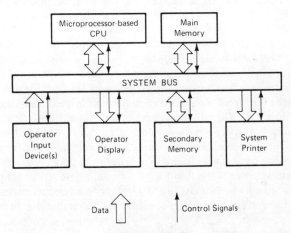

Figure 2-1
A Typical Stand-alone Microcomputer System

3. A *system bus*, the set of wires in the *mother board* (or *backplane* or whatever term the particular manufacturer uses) that carries the signals among the various other subsystems of the microcomputer

4. An *operator input device;* typically this is a typewriter-style *keyboard*, but it may include a device, such as a *mouse*, a *joystick*, a *light pen*, or a *touch-sensitive display screen*, for indicating the location on the display of the information of interest to the operator

5. An *operator visual display*, typically a CRT (TV tube) but possibly some other form of display such as a set of light-emitting diodes (LEDs) or liquid crystal displays in color or monochrome

6. A *secondary memory* slower than the main memory but with greater capacity, such as a *magnetic tape cassette*, one or more *floppy* (or *hard*) *disk(s)* and *drives*, a *videodisc*, a *video tape recorder*, or some combination of the above

7. A *system printer* to produce the "hard copy" that inevitably seems to be needed, possibly including a capability for graphic as well as typed output.

Not shown in the diagram is a vital component, the software; also missing are other possible "peripheral" devices.

The CPU

The CPU is the element of the microcomputer system without which nothing else works. Nonetheless, it is by no means always considered the *most* important. As we shall see in later chapters, the system software can often be of much greater importance. Throughout the late '70s, when microcomputers first made their appearance, 8-bit microprocessors were used in most systems, the most common being the Intel 8080™ series, the Zilog Z80™ (a close relative), the 6502, and the Motorola 6800™ series. These microprocessors are still the most prevalent in 1983, accounting for perhaps 95 percent or more of all microcomputers in operation, possibly because the 8-bit "word" length of these microprocessors suffices to handle the seven-bit character length of the ASCII code used for much of the serial computer communications in the United States (more on that in Chapter 6). The microprocessors of the '70s and early '80s operated under the control of clocks running at 1 to 5 MHz, that is, 1 to 5 million counts per second. The microprocessors themselves do not work that fast since a typical instruction operation consumes from 4 to as many as 20 clock cycles. Thus these microprocessors operate at less than 1 *mips* (for million instructions per second). It is the clock (actually a quartz crystal and some associated electronics) connected to the CPU that serves as the master controller for everything else that happens in the microcomputer.

In the '80s the emphasis will gradually change to the use of more powerful 16- and 32-bit microprocessors, such as the Intel 8086™ series, the Zilog Z8000™, and the Motorola 68000™, which has 32 bits inside and 16 bits at its outside

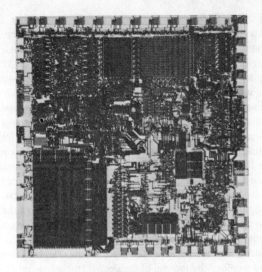

Figure 2-2
Photograph of 8086 Microprocessor
(Courtesy Intel Corporation)

interface; there is also an almost-a-16-bit-microprocessor, the Intel 8088™. These microprocessors follow Moore's law in that they are faster and have more capability than their forebears, the 8-bit processors. The Motorola 68000, for example, packs 68,000 elements onto its chip, compared with 29,000 elements on the Intel 8086 chip (although the chip densities are about the same, around 600,000 elements per square inch). The 68000 also can run with a clock rate of 10 MHz (in the order of 1 to 2 mips). In the mid '80s the 32-bit processor will appear in quantity, making the microcomputer of the late '80s equivalent in power to the small mainframe computers of 1980, but with prices close to those of the microcomputers of today. Hewlett-Packard's 32-bit processor packs 450,000 elements into a chip 0.25 inch on a side. In effect, the huge installation one usually thinks of when the word computer is mentioned will have shrunk to less than the size of the proverbial breadbox. Figure 2-2 shows the details of an 8086 microprocessor.

Main Memory

The main memory is undergoing similar transformations. In the late '70s the typical RAM chip held 1K (computerese for 1024) bits of data, or 128 8-bit "bytes," and a typical RAM memory board was equipped to store 4K bytes. In 1980 the typical RAM chip, such as the 4116, held 2K bytes. Thus a memory board of the same size and with the same number of memory chips as the late '70s board accommodated 64K bytes in 1980, so that the memory was 16 times as dense. In the mid-1980s the 64K-bit chip will be common in low-priced microcomputers. By the late '80s chips holding 256K bits will be the standard. To put this into perspective, an average typed page of text, single-spaced with one-inch margins on 8-1/2″ by 11″ paper, is the equivalent of 3510 bytes, assuming there are no blank lines or line ends. A typical double-spaced page of actual text contains about 1850 bytes. Therefore a single 16K chip can hold a little more than a page of text and a 256K chip will hold almost 18 pages of text. A dozen such chips would be able to hold the entire contents of this book with room to spare. If the book were to be set up in electronic form, stored on a magnetic disk or a videodisc, and if it were also to be set up in a data base format rather than the linear, indexed way in which printed books are usually produced, then the typical reader of the late '80s could easily access any portion of the book essentially instantaneously—letting the computer take care of the "page" flipping. One might also recompile various sections of the book to suit an immediate purpose, such as putting all the material referring to modems in a single reference file or, for that matter, putting all the material from several books on modems in one reference file. Since all the searching would be within the high speed memory (by the end of the decade) the whole process might only take a few seconds or less.

The part of the memory that is easily alterable by the operator consists of RAM chips. ROM (non-alterable) chips of various sorts are also important in many systems, particularly when they contain software that is used frequently, such as a language interpreter, a system monitor, or (a case of interest in this book) a telecommunications controller. The most important distinction between a RAM and a ROM chip is that the ROM chip is non-volatile. That is, it *does not forget* when the power is turned off. A RAM chip forgets instantly when the power goes. The disadvantage of ROM is that, in general, its reaction time is slower than RAM, typically four to five times as long. As this decade progresses, ROM chips will get faster and RAM boards will more frequently include battery backup power supplies to keep the higher speed memories intact after the main power is turned off. Erasable ROMs of various sorts will evolve so that, by the end of the '80s at the latest, most microcomputers will have substantial amounts of high-speed erasable ROMs, providing both power-off stability and rapid response.

The System Bus

The reason that the system bus is shown as open-ended on the right side of Figure 2-1 is that most microcomputer systems, except at the very lowest-price end of the market, have some capability for expansion of the basic set of components. This is accomplished either through the inclusion of additional "slots" on the system bus for installation of more component "boards" or by the provision of an additional expansion module serving the same purpose. Some computers, even in the higher price ranges, may not have this expansion capability. Since it is required for use with telecommunications systems, the wise buyer will make sure that the microcomputer is expandable (or already has telecommunications capability) before purchasing it.

Although the majority of computers in use today do not conform to a standard system bus, there are many which use a bus known as the S-100 or IEEE-696 bus. The S-100 bus got its name from the fact that it contains 100 conductors for signal and power connections among the system circuit boards. The standard is such that microcomputers using either 8-bit or 16-bit words can operate using it. Both 8-bit and 16-bit versions use the same 16 wires in the bus. The 8-bit mode uses 8 of the wires to send data from the CPU to the other boards, the other 8 wires to receive data from the boards (memory, controllers, etc.). The 16-bit mode uses the wires bidirectionally—both to send and to receive data. Most of the other wires in the S-100 bus are used for control signals between the CPU and the other components of the system.

The virtue of a standard bus, from the user's point of view, is that a microcomputer system using it can be gradually upgraded or rearranged to suit changing requirements simply by changing or adding circuit boards that plug into the bus. Another "standard" bus is the Intel *Multibus* which is frequently used in microcomputers with industrial control applications.

Finally, there is another standard bus that is important, although it is not a system bus in the sense that we are using the term here. It is the IEEE-488 bus, used for communication between microcomputers and instrumentation that is external to the microcomputer. One popular 1980-vintage microcomputer series, the Commodore PET and its progeny, uses the IEEE-488 as a standard means of communicating with the external world. That particular bus will get more attention in a later chapter.

Operator Input Devices

The microcomputer is totally useless if it can not accept information from its operator in some form easily manageable for a human. The typewriter-like keyboard is by far the most common means of operator data input to a microcomputer. Most microcomputers use QWERTY-arranged keyboards (that is, with the keys laid out like the common typewriter), for traditional rather than rational reasons. These standard alphanumeric keys are surrounded by varying assortments of special keys. Most of the special keys produce control signals, or sequences of them, that are used by the microcomputer to perform special, untypewriter-like functions. This, too, will be treated in greater detail in later chapters.

A growing number of microcomputers are also using special devices for operator input. The most popular class of these input augmentors includes the "mouse" and "joystick" devices used to convey position information to the computer. A mouse is a small box with a ball bearing or a set of wheels on its bottom and a control switch or two on its top. As the operator moves the mouse back, forth, up, or down on a desk top it signals the movement to the microcomputer. The microcomputer reacts by changing the position on the operator's display of the *cursor* (the blinking spot, arrow, underline bar, or other indicator of "where" the operator is in the computer's main memory). A joystick is used in the same general way. The joystick is essentially a rod sticking out of a small control box. The box end of the rod is attached to a ball bearing like that used in the mouse. The other end can be moved around the ball pivot to indicate direction. The difference between the joystick and the mouse is that the joystick changes the direction and speed of movement of the cursor while the mouse directly changes the cursor location.

"Light pens" and "touch-sensitive display screens" are similar in their action to the mouse. The light pen contains a small photodetector. When the operator puts the tip of the pen up against the display screen and pushes the accompanying button (or presses on the tip) the computer "reads" the location of the pen by comparing the timing of the pulse of light detected by the pen with the known position of the electron beam that is "writing" the images on the display. The display screen is written in a serial fashion, that is, starting at the upper left corner of the screen, moving to the upper right corner, quickly going back to the left margin of the next line, writing to the right margin, and so on. Thus each point on the surface of the screen can be associated with a unique instant in time, which the light pen detects. Most touch-sensitive displays use a matrix of either LED/photodiodes or transparent capacitor arrays to detect a physical touch such as a finger on the display screen. These sensors directly produce the information about the screen position; the light-pen systems require that the position be derived. Graphics tablets work in a fashion similar to the touch-sensitive displays.

Operator Visual Display

The operator visual display is usually a TV-tube-like CRT (Cathode Ray Tube). In fact, most of the lower-priced microcomputers use the owner's TV as the operator display. The problem with a TV set is that it has insufficient visual resolution, because of its small video bandwidth, to produce high-quality displays. High-resolution displays use larger video bandwidths, up to 30 MHz or more (as contrasted with 3 to 6 MHz in a TV set) and cost more as a consequence. The current need to use a CRT as the display device is a limiting factor in reducing display cost; it is quite difficult to make the displays less expensively than they are made now. The best hope for significant cost reduction in this aspect of the microcomputer system is the practical development of another technique entirely, such as large liquid-crystal displays. Liquid crystals are the displays used in many pocket calculators and digital watches.

Secondary Memory

Secondary memory is significantly slower than main memory, with access times measured in tens of milliseconds rather than hundreds of nanoseconds (a nanosecond is one-billionth of a second). Secondary memory also has much higher capacity than main memory, is non-volatile, and is less expensive per bit stored. Therefore, secondary memory systems are ordinarily used for the "library" function in a microcomputer system, storing data, programs, text, and other information for access by the main memory as needed. Typical secondary memory units are audio tape cassettes, tape cartridges, floppy disks, hard disks, video discs and video tape recorders. Each different medium for secondary memory requires a different "controller," a specialized set of microelectronics for handling the details of reading and writing the data for that type of secondary memory unit. The controller is most often located in the microcomputer system box but can also be incorporated in the secondary memory unit itself. The capacity of the secondary memory can range from about 80K bytes, in the case of a single-sided single-density minifloppy disk, to billions of bytes, in the case of a videodisc. As with most of the other components of the microcomputer, the price for a given level of capacity of secondary memory is steadily going down (or the capacity for a given price is steadily going up). The rate of capacity improvement is just slightly lower than the rate of microelectronics improvement.

System Printer

The capacity of the operator display is inadequate for many information-processing functions. Frequently the operator wants to be able to review several or many pages of text during the course of a session with the computer. For this purpose some form of printer is generally required. There are three main determinants of the cost of a printer: speed, print quality, and flexibility. The least expensive type of contemporary printer uses a matrix of dots to form letters. The visual clarity of the results is proportional to the number of dots in the matrix: the more dots there are, the better the quality. At the other end of the speed-quality-flexibility spectrum are laser printers that can turn out thousands of pages per hour with typeset quality. In between are various forms of fixed-font printers of which the daisy-wheel or thimble printers are the most familiar to microcomputer system users. These printers take their names from the shapes of their print elements. Dot-matrix printers are approaching the quality of the daisy-wheel and thimble-element printers—at one-fourth to one-third the price—but currently still produce character shapes not quite good enough to satisfy the correspondence needs of many users. Most printers in the under-$5000 category are not as fast as operator displays; they are often the limiting factor in the rate at which data can be accepted over a telecommunications line when immediate printout is required.

Other Peripherals

A number of other "peripheral devices" can be plugged into empty slots of most commercially available microcomputers and/or their extension boxes. These include clock cards to keep track of the time and date, various high-resolution computer graphics cards for drawing pictures, special cards to convert from the primary, ROM-based language of the microcomputer (such as BASIC) to other languages (such as PASCAL), and, most important, for the purposes of this book, cards for telecommunication. For the most part, telecommunication capability is an extra in contemporary microcomputers. Only the ability to communicate with the operator console (keyboard and display), and possibly with an external device or two such as a printer, is normally included in most of the lower-priced microcomputers. In the lowest-priced sets the printer connection is an extra-cost option.

As the heading of this section suggests, most microcomputers are designed basically as stand-alone units. Their capacity must be extended for them to become able to telecommunicate.

COMMUNICATIONS TERMINALS

Often, the reason one wishes to have a microcomputer that communicates is to allow it to have access to a larger computer in another location. The larger computer may be used to run programs that are beyond the capacity of the microcomputer, it may be used as the repository of a large database, or it may serve as a node in a widespread telecommunications network. In this sense the microcomputer is, however temporarily, part of a *distributed processing system*. Part of the information processing is done by the microcomputer, part by another computer or computers. A majority of those who first purchased microcomputers for telecommunications expected to use them in this manner.

With increasing frequency the microcomputer is taking the place of the larger computer of a few years ago, if on a smaller scale. The microcomputer is serving as the "mainframe" and is communicating with "smart" or "dumb" terminals elsewhere. This seems reasonable since contemporary microcomputers have the power of mainframes of a decade ago. Often the operator-input and display capabilities are contained within a separate terminal external to the main box of the microcomputer. A "dumb" terminal contains only those basic capabilities: a keyboard and a display with its associated power supply, alphanumeric character generator, and display memory. A "smart" terminal does other things as well. The functions it performs can range from additional graphics for the display, through sending and receiving strings of characters at a single keystroke, to such powerful ones that the terminal is a full-fledged microcomputer able, if necessary, to operate on its own.

One form of smart terminal contains its own semipermanent memory. The terminal can be used, for example, by a salesperson to collect order information from customers during the day. The information is stored in a magnetic "bubble" memory or in an electronic memory with battery-supported memory-keeping capability. At the end of the day the salesperson can dial up the computer at the central office and "dump" the order information without going to the office. During the dump, the information accumulated in the memory is read to the central computer via the telephone coupler built into the terminal. See Chapter 6 for more details on the hardware.

The terminal user need not be a salesperson 2,000 miles away. A typical use for a remote terminal is order entry or inventory maintenance. Here the terminal may be in the same building or even the same room. It can be connected to the *host* microcomputer via a direct cable or by a telephone connection such as an intercom system. Either way, the computational workload is carried by the microcomputer.

Keep in mind, however, that most personal computers come with an *operating system* designed for a single user—that is, the software that controls the internal functions of the computer (the operating system) is designed for operation in a stand-alone mode. In order to get such a computer to operate with more than one terminal simultaneously, the addition of a multi-user operating system is usually necessary. For simple tasks, a single-user operating system can work with another terminal via a modem interface. In this way the operating system is fooled into thinking that the extra terminal is just another I/O device. However, in this mode of operation, the two terminals cannot be used simultaneously.

INTELLIGENT DEVICES

Microprocessors are also used extensively in non-computer devices. Perhaps the most prevalent examples of this use are automobile fuel-injection control systems and microwave ovens. In most such intelligent devices the purpose of the microprocessor is to replace or surpass complicated electromechanical parts such as timers, gear trains, relays, cams, and the like. If a microprocessor and associated electronics can do the job less expensively or better than the mechanical alternative, it may be chosen as a key element in the device.

Scientific instruments are another group of devices that are increasingly being made more intelligent by the use of microprocessors. They are also becoming more communicative, relaying their information directly to computers (including microcomputers) for direct analysis. In fact, it was because of the large and growing number of communicating scientific instruments that the IEEE General Purpose Interface Bus (GPIB), better known as the IEEE-488 bus, was developed. There is also a comparable international standard for interfacing programmable digital instruments.

The devices mentioned above are essentially stand-alone in their present stage of development, although ones such as electronic ignition systems often come with special communications ports so that specialized instruments can talk to them for diagnostic purposes. These devices, as is, are not of much interest from the viewpoint of microcomputer communications; nevertheless they may be the beginning of a trend in which increasing numbers of devices will have communications capability with other devices and computers for both diagnostic and control purposes.

For example, while microwave ovens include an increasing number of programmable features, none are available that can be reprogrammed remotely (by telephone)—yet. As the costs of microelectronic components continue to decrease, however, it is reasonable to expect that such communicating ovens, as well as a variety of other devices, will be commonplace. A significant portion of the time of a typical house computer in the latter part of this century will be spent monitoring various smart devices. These will be used to improve security, energy consumption, lawn and garden maintenance and, possibly at the top of the list, home entertainment. Smart devices are already being used for home lighting control, although the prices of the controllers are still substantially higher than the basic mechanical light switch. Prices will come down, in relative terms, and the number of applications of such controllers will increase in direct proportion to the decrease in prices.

Part of the bill for lowering the prices through "learning curve"* effects will be paid during the growth in the use of microelectronic control systems and associated specialized sensors in automobiles.

---

*The term "learning curve" refers to the process of adding improvements to the product as production experience accumulates. Typically the product is said to improve X percent (usually by reduction of its cost) each time production doubles. In the microelectronics industry the learning factor, X, is about 30 percent.

3

Most owners of personal computers are interested in communicating with other computers located at a considerable distance from them. That is, their main interest in telecommunications cannot be satisfied by stringing a cable between their own computer and another in the same room or a few rooms away, although that topic will be treated later. The primary medium for most of this desired form of long-distance communication is the telephone.

TELEPHONES

The telephone is the only two-way telecommunications system with which most of us have extensive experience. There are other familiar forms of telecommunications, of course, such as TV and radio, but most of those are broadcast systems. Being one-way, they are unsuitable for getting responses from the listeners. There are also two-way forms of radio and two-way TV-like systems such as Citizens' Band (CB) radio and Picturephone™, but these do not have anything close to the level of use of the telephone. Most of us do not even think twice about using a telephone. It represents an almost invisible technology— blends into the woodwork, so to speak.

One of the reasons the telephone is so familiar to most of us is that it is such a highly developed and perfected technology. Even the least noxious "bugs" have been nearly eradicated, and the result is that the system works very smoothly indeed. We *expect* to hear a dial tone when we pick up the receiver. We *expect* to hear a ring at the other end in response to our dialing. We *expect* to hear the person at the other end clearly when the telephone is answered. When one of these expectations is not met, we are irritated, even incensed. We do not realize what an extensive technological system the telephone system is. The following is an overview of the basic concepts of operation of the telephone system, a review of all those things that are happening unnoticed by us as we telephone someone else. The basic steps in completing a telephone transaction are covered in some detail because they are identical to many of the steps in computer telecommunications.

Beginnings

The first telephone communicated only between rooms in Alexander Graham Bell's workshop. A pair of wires connected the two speaking instruments. For the first few years of commercial telephony the situation was much the same.

Telecommunications Systems

Individuals wanting to telephone others had to arrange an individual telephone hookup. For instance, if you wanted to have a telephone between your home and your business office you would buy a pair of telephones: one for the house and one for the office. You would then connect a pair of wires between the two, add a set of batteries to power them, and be in operation. Of course, that was the only communications path you could use. There was no way you could talk to Aunt Martha with that system.

Naturally, once the idea of the telephone caught on, all sorts of people wanted to have them. One of the photographs of downtown Manhattan taken toward the end of the last century shows mazes of wires running among buildings, interconnecting all those individual telephone circuits—a form of wire pollution. Clearly, things were getting out of hand. In response to this problem the party line and the telephone switchboard made their appearance (see Figure 3-1).

THE INTRODUCTION OF TELEPHONE NETWORKS. Instead of having individual sets of lines strung between each pair of subscribers, the idea was accepted of connecting several subscribers to a single main line. This was particularly attractive in rural areas where the cost of duplicate sets of wires running long distances between farms was prohibitive. The result was the party line. This, of course, brought on its own technological problem, as well as a new form of entertainment on those long winter evenings. How was the callee supposed to know he or she was being called when several people shared the same line?

The answer to that difficulty was a system of ringing codes. At the time, the individual telephone systems were still battery-powered. A bell was added to each telephone, along with a hand-cranked magneto. If, in Figure 3-1b, subscriber A wished to call subscriber B, A would crank the magneto according to B's code, say two shorts and a long. B would then pick up the receiver and the conversation would begin, possibly modified by the fact that D was sure to be eavesdropping. Of course, before calling someone else one was supposed to listen briefly to make sure that no one else was using the system before ringing up one's intended callee.

The party-line system works reasonably well as long as there are relatively few subscribers connected to the line and/or their messages are quite short. In those cases the problems of *line contention* (several different pairs of subscribers wanting to use the line at the same time) are small. As more people acquired telephones and as their use of them increased, line contention problems grew correspondingly. A number of other social issues became important as well. For instance, chief executives did not want others listening in on discussions of business prospects, and doctors wanted direct access to hospitals without the

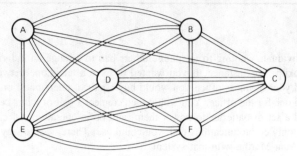

(a)   Individual Private Lines

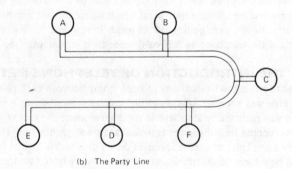

(b)   The Party Line

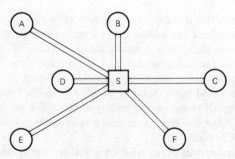

(c)   The Star-connected Switchboard

Figure 3-1
Early Telephone Terms

delays imposed by the party-line structure. The switchboard and the star connection system solved those problems.

In Figure 3-1c the subscribers are all interconnected by a switchboard. All of the telephone lines run to the switchboard instead of to individual homes or offices. In the first switchboard systems, the caller would ring up the switchboard, somewhat as on a party line, with an identifying ring signal. The operator would then plug a jack into the receptacle corresponding to the subscriber's telephone line in order to connect his or her earphones to the caller. The caller would tell the operator the name or number of the person being called. The operator would pick up the jack associated with the callee's telephone and plug it into the caller's position on the switchboard, then ring the callee's line (with the proper code if it was a party line). The connection was thus completed and the call could progress if the callee answered. When the conversation was completed the two parties would ring the operator to signal that the jacks could be unplugged; they would "ring off."

As the technology grew more sophisticated more innovations were added. First, the telephone company provided a single central battery for powering the telephones, replacing the individual subscriber batteries. By continually sensing the current in a subscriber's line the company could automatically tell when the telephone was "off hook," that is, ready to communicate. The off-hook signal would cause a light to glow and a buzzer to sound on the operator's switchboard, signifying that a call was incoming. A similar system would sense that one or both callers had "hung up" (that is, had hung the earphone of the telephone on its hook) so that the lines could be disconnected.

A Technological Digression: Many of the terms invented to describe the operation of the telephone persist today and will still be found by the person trying to connect a computer to a telephone line (see Figure 3-2). In addition to the terms "on-" and "off-hook," "hang up," "ring up," "ring off," "switchboard," and others to be covered later, the wires in the telephone line have their own particular identification. The plug used in a switchboard has two conductors: the tip, which is connected to the positive voltage side of the line, and the ring, which is connected to the negative side of the line. These terms are still used to identify the wires in the telephone although the use of the plug-in switchboard has almost disappeared.

The Rise of Automation

The history of technology is fraught with very nontechnological reasons for innovation, and telephone technology has its own practical hero. The inventor of the automatic telephone switching system that was first to gain widespread acceptance was an undertaker. Almon P. Strowger was one of only two undertakers in the small town in which he lived. Nothing remarkable in that. However, there was one technological problem: the wife of the other undertaker was also the town telephone operator. When someone called on the telephone and asked

(a) On-Hook, Off-Hook, Hang up

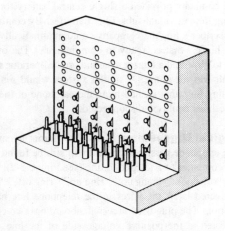

(b) Switchboard

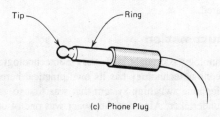

(c) Phone Plug

Figure 3-2
Some Telephone Systems

for an undertaker, the operator somehow seemed to have a bias in favor of her husband, to the detriment of Strowger's business. Strowger was irresistably motivated to find a way to automate the town telephone switchboard. The rotary switch mechanism he invented and sold to the Automatic Electric Company in the late nineteenth century is still to be found in large numbers of telephone switching centers throughout the world. Strowger's business picked up as well, once his life and death problem had been solved.

The next problem, once the automatic connector riddle was solved, was that of arranging automatic signalling and ringing. This was done by the familiar rotary dial on the telephone which rotates at a uniform rate, interrupting the telephone current as it goes past each number dialed. That is, if a five is dialed, the dial will interrupt the current as it goes past five, four, three, two, and one, at a rate of ten pulses per second. (Strictly speaking, the rate must be between 8 and 10 pulses per second.) In the last two decades the tone-signalling system has begun to supplant the pulse system. An individual number or signal character in the tone-signalling system is a combination of a pair of sinusoidal tones rather than a pulsed interruption in the telephone current (more on that in Chapter 5). The advantage of the tone-dialing system is not that it sounds more musical but that it can be more than ten times faster than the pulsed system. Dialing time is slightly more than one second per number dialed in a pulsed system; it can be as little as one-tenth of a second per number dialed in a tone system.

Once the switching center has detected that a caller is off-hook it connects a dial tone signal to the caller's line. On the average, that takes about 1/10 second. Once the dialing sequence is completed the next bank of switches connects the caller's line to that of the callee and starts the ring signals. By the way, the ring signal you hear in your telephone earpiece is not the signal that is causing the ringing at the other end; they are independently generated and are not necessarily in synchronism. When the callee answers, the automatic billing equipment starts timing the call after a brief delay (less than 2 seconds), then ceases timing when one of the parties hangs up. Each line is disconnected when the party hangs up. If one party fails to hang up, or fails to dial within a preset period, an off-hook signal is sent to the errant party.

These are the basic components and processes in the telephone system: individual telephones *(handsets)* with dials or numbered buttons; and switching centers for supplying the basic electrical power, performing the switching, and generating the dial-tone, ring, busy and off-hook signals. This basic pattern can be repeated and expanded to cover anything from a self-contained local telephone system serving only a few telephones to an international network linking millions of instruments.

For example, suppose that you are trying to phone someone at a great distance, such as from San Francisco to New York. The procedure is roughly similar to that of making a local call but with some additions. The noticeable change is that you add four numbers to the number of the person (or computer) you are calling. These numbers signify whether you are calling direct or require some form of operator intervention (the leading "1" or "0" in the long-distance telephone number) and to what area of the country—or the world—you are calling (the area code). At the local switching exchange these leading numbers cause the equipment to switch to a long distance rather than a local line. This line is called a *trunk* (I don't know how it got that name except, possibly, that the line is thick and covered with a gray coat—like an elephant's trunk). A trunk connects two switching centers. There may be a series of subsequent connections made between different switching centers as your telephone dialing directions work their way across the country, none of which are explicitly called in the number you dialed. The decision about which centers are interconnected to get your call from San Francisco to New York is internal to the telephone system itself. The only way in which the process is made evident to the caller is that there are additional delays, and perhaps some muted signalling tones, as these connections are made. The links between switching centers may be wires (just like the local connection between your telephone or computer and the switching center), overland microwave relays, or a communication satellite. After all these long-distance links have been made, your call goes into the local exchange in New York and is treated there like any other local call. Even though the technology used over the long-distance link may be more spectacular than the switches and wires used for the local distribution, the underlying principles are the same.

The expansion of the local, two-party telephone system to international scale has been made possible by the development of national and international standards for telephone transmission. Without these standards each private telephone system and each individual telephone company might have equipment incompatible with that of the others. Such incompatibility would not be a problem if people wanted to use telephones only within their own particular systems. Clearly, many people wish to be able to communicate with essentially anyone, anywhere, anytime. For this to be possible, the standards were required. The result is that there are few places that cannot now be reached by telephone, even though one or more of the links may be by radio. In principle then, there are few places that cannot be interconnected by telecommunicating computers. This question of standards will come up repeatedly during later chapters.

POWER UTILITIES

Telephone systems are not the only means of computer telecommunications. Another means of telecommunications is hidden right under our noses or, better, in our walls: the electrical power system. Actually the electrical power utility companies have been using their power lines for decades to communicate "housekeeping" information between central power stations. None of this communication gets to the individual consumer of electricity. The form of power-system communication of greatest interest to the microcomputer user is that of device control.

The theory is simple. The house or office wiring system offers the same fundamental resource as does the telephone system—pairs of wires. The fact that these wires carry high voltages certainly complicates the matter but it does not vitiate the basic fact that the resource is there. The problem is that any signals used for telecommunications must somehow be isolated from the main purpose of the power lines, carrying power. Once this is accomplished the wires can be used in the same way that telephone wires are used. Microcomputers can send and receive messages to each other and/or to devices connected to the same power lines.

The chief virtue of this is that an existing facility, the home, office or laboratory wiring, can act as a communications path, thereby eliminating the need for additional wiring for many control-system applications to be discussed later. The difficulty is that isolation of the communications system from interference generated in the power system may not always be simple. Nevertheless, microcomputer-based device-control systems are available in today's market and can be expected to become more popular as the technology improves and gets less expensive and as standards develop for these systems.

CABLE TV

Community Access TeleVision (CATV) systems, better known as cable TV, have made steady growth since their first appearance in the 1950s. First popular in rural areas where the TV signals from distant cities were too weak for the home TV receiver and simple antenna, cable systems have spread recently to the major cities. Now, in addition to the standard commercial broadcast signals, the new cable systems provide many other entertainment and information channels. Although this doesn't seem to have much to do with microcomputers there is a connection.

At present most cable TV is broadcast only. That is, the signals are sent from the "head end" of the system, where the main transmitter is located, to the individual subscribers. In a few years, if the present market trends continue, most large cable TV systems will be bidirectional. The subscribers will be able to send signals back to the head end of the system. One of the first extended experiments in this use of cable is the Warner Qube system in Columbus, Ohio, begun in the late 1970s. The Qube system had a very simple subscriber-response terminal and did not even approximate the complexity of a contemporary communicating microcomputer. Nevertheless it demonstrated that a two-way cable system could work.

As microcomputers enter the telecommunications arena we can expect them to be connected to cable systems as key elements in a number of business and consumer *network information service* functions. A network information service is a service to consumers (of various sorts) performed by an organization that uses a telecommunications medium as its means of providing the service. For example, the information operator employed by the telephone company provides a network information service. The Dow Jones stock quotations and the weather forecasts displayed on one of the cable TV channels are two more. In the case of the telephone operator the service is *interactive*. You give the operator specific instructions concerning the information you want. In the case of the stock quotations and weather forecasts the service is *broadcast* only. You must wait until the information you are seeking comes by.

This difference between interactive and broadcast services may be a crucial one in years to come. As the information society grows more complex our information needs will become more specialized. The ability of general-purpose information media, such as newspapers or broadcasts, to solve our specific information needs will diminish as the time we have to spend on them diminishes. More frequently we will be searching for specific kinds of information and looking for more effective ways to skim through the vast supply of other information to find what we want. We will become impatient with the cable system as a provider of stock quotations; we will want to know about the stocks we are interested in *right now!* We will want to get the comparative shopping figures at the various neighborhood markets arranged so that they correspond to today's shopping list, preferably with a map of the markets showing the aisles in which the items are located. In order to do this we will need something more sophisticated than a simple push-button box connected to the TV set and the cable system.

We will need some form of microcomputer to keep records for us and to transmit and receive the information over the cable system for these more sophisticated capabilities. Such systems were not widely available at the end of 1982 but will become more so as the decade—and the cable systems—develop. By 1990 it is likely that a number of interactive network information utilities will be available over cable systems. Some of these will be nationally available, such as specialized news services; others will be tailored to individual cable communities and specific groups of subscribers, as in the supermarket example above.

There will be several years during the next decades in which some interesting competition will occur among various means of providing network information services. The telephone systems have the potential lead at the moment since many services are already provided over telephone lines, as will be discussed in later chapters. But cable and other non-switching systems also are developing comparable or even superior capabilities as the technology improves. For example, cable systems could provide information to microcomputers at higher rates than are possible with contemporary twisted-pair telephone systems, simply because they can operate at much greater *bandwidths** than the audio-limited

---

* Bandwidth is a prime characteristic of a communications channel. The greater the bandwidth, the greater the amount of information that can be sent down it in a given interval of time. A standard TV channel has a bandwidth of 6 MHz, or 6 million cycles per second. A standard telephone line (if transmitted as single-sideband AM) has a bandwidth of about 3 KHz, so 2,000 telephone conversations could squeeze into a single TV channel, although with a little crosstalk.

telephones. (It turns out that the telephone companies have some similar tricks up their sleeves.)

Rate of transmission may be important in some applications, such as the transmission of programs to subscriber microcomputers. Imagine ordering the latest program for deciphering your income tax while taking as many legal deductions as possible. This might easily be communicated to you via your local cable system, possibly after the late, late, late show, when there are few customers to serve. (Naturally with no difficulty you would have programmed your personal computer to accept the transmission while you slept.) It might be much more time-consuming to transmit a long program through the audio bandwidth of the telephone system—perhaps as much as 2000 times as long. Of course, there are ways to speed up the telephone transmission, and there are reasons that cable transmission may not be that fast, but the rate of transmission required will influence the types of network information services provided through the different media.

For cable systems, as for microcomputers themselves and for the telephone system, there exists a need to establish some common basis for communication and some common means of connecting to the systems, or the chances are fairly good that no useful communication will occur. Each cable network, each microcomputer system, each telephone network with its own, mutually incompatible, set of signalling conventions could make the entire assemblage an expensive way of hindering communication or at best of splitting the world up into numerous little isolated groups. It is unlikely, however, that this terrible situation will come to pass, because there are so many pressures for increasing rather than restricting the flow of communications. Nevertheless, there are existing variances between communications systems that can cause difficulty for those wishing to have free access to a variety of communications media.

WIRELESS COMMUNICATIONS

Up to now we have been considering only communications over wires of some sort: the telegraph, the telephone, network cables, and house-wiring systems. But telecommunication is not restricted to systems that use wires to carry the messages. A variety of wireless communication systems are available and will probably be used for carrying communications to microcomputers in the future. Some of them are in use now. These will be explored more fully in later chapters.

Technical Principles

The principles of wireless communication are the same for all the forms in common use today: radio, TV, and microwave. These different types of wireless telecommunication differ primarily in the frequencies used, and in some of the particular properties that are frequency-dependent. The *modulation* techniques (the ways by which the message is packaged into the communications medium, or carrier) are also similar for the various types of wireless transmission systems, and similar to those used for systems using wires. In fact, the primary difference between a telecommunications system using wires and one that does not is some extra complication in the latter.

That complication is due to the fact that empty space, once thought of as containing an invisible "ether," needs some coaxing before it will accept messages for communication to some other place. In principle, space will gladly accept signals at any frequency and carry them anywhere at the speed of light. In practice a few other things have to be done. The most important of these is that the signals must be launched and received properly, via antennas of some sort. The key point is that free space is sensitive to the dimensions of things, in this case the *wavelength* of the signals being sent. So the antenna used to transmit or receive a signal must be of a size appropriate for that wavelength.

The wavelength can easily be calculated for a signal of some arbitrary frequency. It is the speed of light divided by the frequency of the signal in Hertz (cycles per second). The speed of light is roughly 300,000,000 meters per second. The frequency of the alternating current in your electrical power line is either 50 Hz or 60 Hz, depending on where you live. Therefore the wavelength of your electrical power signal is 300,000,000 divided by 60 or 5 million meters. A good antenna should be a reasonable fraction of a wavelength in size to transmit efficiently. Bigger is better. A quarter-wavelength of your electrical power signal is about 780 miles. Not much sense in using that to transmit wireless signals (although it is a problem for long-distance power lines). It is much better to use signals at millions or even billions of Hertz so that the antennas can be of reasonable size.

For example, the center frequency of TV channel 6 is 85 MHz (million Hertz, or megaHertz). Its wavelength is 300,000,000 divided by 85,000,000 or about 3.5 meters. A half-wavelength antenna, which is reasonably efficient, would be 1.76 meters long (69 inches). That is much easier to deal with. The reason we appear to be digressing into topics that do not seem to be directly related to telecommunications between computers is that, if you plan to look into wireless communications of some sort, one of the first things to be considered is the required or optimum size of the needed equipment. In contrast to the microelectronics revolution, there does not seem to be any way to miniaturize space. A half-wavelength antenna designed to transmit most efficiently in the middle of channel 6 has to be 1.76 meters long even if the rest of the equipment attached to it is the size of a postage stamp. When you use wires for the transmission you avoid that problem.

One other factor of importance in wireless communications is also related to frequency. In most forms of telecommunications used today the message being sent is superimposed on a higher-frequency signal known as the *carrier*. The reason for this goes back to the antenna argument. You may want to telecommunicate using a signal at 200 MHz so that you can use a relatively small antenna but you do not have 200 million items per second to send. So you superimpose your message, which is at a much lower frequency—say, 1200 Hz—on the 200

MHz carrier. This process uses up a few frequencies near 200 MHz. In the most simple case, not so simply called double-sideband amplitude modulation, you will need to use the frequencies between 199.9988 MHz and 200.0012 MHz in order to transmit your signal. The difference between those two frequencies is known as the *bandwidth* of the signal. In this case it turns out to be exactly twice the frequency of the message being transmitted. That is, the bandwidth of the transmitted signal is 2400 Hz while the original message is at 1200 Hz.

A Technical Digression: By the way, this concept of bandwidth is not unique to wireless communications. All signals have this property of bandwidth, regardless of their primary frequency. A quality stereo system has a bandwidth of at least 20,000 Hz. The telephone has a bandwidth of about 2700 Hz, adequate for intelligible voice transmission. Your eye has a bandwidth of about 370 trillion Hz (370,000,000,000,000 Hz), the visible spectrum. The reason bandwidth is important is that the frequency space occupied by a signal, its bandwidth, determines how many similar but unrelated signals can be packed next to each other near the same center frequency. If you are communicating at a fairly low rate, such as 1200 Hz, you do not use much frequency space. If you are communicating at a fairly high rate, like that used by a TV signal— several million Hertz—you need a considerable amount of space, so much that you cannot even consider transmitting at a frequency less than 5 MHz or so. Aside from the antenna problem, this is another reason (beside antenna size) that the commercial TV broadcast band runs from 54 MHz (channel 2) to 890 MHz (channel 83). Each channel has a bandwidth of 6 MHz.

Now that we have ground through the preliminaries we can briefly examine some of the existing and future wireless telecommunications options for microcomputers.

Radio

Radio was the first form of wireless telecommunication. The era of the radio was ushered in by Marconi's first intercontinental transmission between England and France in 1898. For a few decades the predominant form of radio telecommunications was what is known as CW (continuous wave) transmission. This is the radio equivalent of the telegraph. The carrier signal is turned on and off in a manner analogous to the sending of voltage pulses down a telegraph wire. In 1906, as a result of the invention of the triode vacuum tube by Lee DeForest, it became possible to transmit voices over the "airwaves" using "amplitude modulation" of the carrier (more on that shortly). Commercial broadcast radio thus became possible. Using carrier frequencies between 0.535 MHz and 1.605 MHz in the United States, *AM* (amplitude modulation) broadcast stations sprang up all over the country to deliver news and entertainment to the home.

As technology progressed other forms of modulation became possible. One of the major difficulties with amplitude modulation is that it is quite susceptible to noise from a number of sources: lightning, electrical equipment, automobile ignition systems, whatever emits electrical energy at the frequencies used in the telecommunications. A form of modulation that is considerably less susceptible to interference of this type is *FM* (frequency modulation). Figure 3-3 illustrates the differences. In Figure 3-3a the two major components of a wireless signal are shown separately: the message signal, simply called the signal, and the carrier. The carrier is at a frequency higher than the maximum frequency of the signal; usually it is at a considerably higher frequency, as we have seen.

In amplitude modulation, Figure 3-3b, the signal is impressed on the carrier in such a way as to change the instantaneous voltage or power of the carrier; the frequency of the carrier is unchanged. In frequency modulation the instantaneous power of the carrier is unaltered from what it would be if there were no signal. Instead, the frequency of the carrier is changed to correspond to the instantaneous voltage of the signal, as is shown in Figure 3-3c. A large value of the signal voltage produces a large shift in the frequency of the carrier, up to 75 KHz (75,000 cycles per second) added to, or subtracted from, the carrier frequency in commercial FM broadcasting in the US. In AM transmission the bandwidth of the combined signal is twice the highest frequency of the message signal, or about 10 KHz (2 × 5,000 Hz) for commercial broadcasts in the United States. In FM transmission the minimum bandwidth required is twice the maximum *deviation* of the signal from the nominal carrier frequency, or 150 KHz in the United States. (The actual bandwidth of commercial FM is 225 KHz.) Because FM signals need more bandwidth than do AM signals, they are transmitted with higher carrier frequencies so that a reasonable number of different signals can occupy a given percentage of radio spectrum.

TV and Microwave

The same technical principles apply to television signals as apply to radio signals. TV signals, at least the picture-carrying part of them, use amplitude modulation. The sound portion of a TV transmission uses FM, transmitted over a "subcarrier" 4.5 MHz higher than the carrier of the picture signal. For color TV, there is also a color subcarrier, making the composite signal fairly complicated. However, these details are not of major importance to telecommunicating *microcomputers*, except in that they illustrate the fact that the bandwidth required by computer data transmission is quite small compared with that used by these standard broadcast telecommunications media.

The term *microwave* is used to cover a large portion of the electromagnetic spectrum, the portion generally above the TV band but below the frequencies of light. In practice, the microwave band runs from about 1 GHz (for *gigaHertz* or 1,000 MHz) to about 300 GHz (visible light starts at about 400,000 GHz in the deep red). Most microwave data transmission occurs in the low end of that band. The higher reaches are used by the military, and for exotic purposes such as deep-space communications. One of the primary commercial uses of the microwave band is in the transmission of telephone and data signals over long distances. When it became possible in the late 1940s and early 1950s to transmit

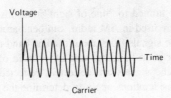

Carrier

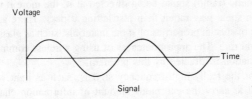

Signal

(a) The Two Components

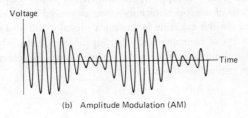

(b) Amplitude Modulation (AM)

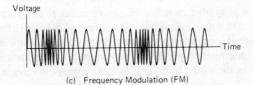

(c) Frequency Modulation (FM)

Figure 3-3
Types of Modulation

microwave signals reliably, the ease of long-distance communication was greatly enhanced. The cost of transmission was also reduced because it was no longer necessary to install thousands of miles of wires to carry the signals.

There is one limitation to FM, TV, and microwave transmission that is important in considerations of the possible range of a telecommunications link.

These frequencies are limited to "line of sight" transmission. Signals at lower frequencies, such as are used in AM radio, can bend around the earth's surface to some extent, but the signals from about the FM band upward are stopped by such things as hills or even buildings and other solid objects. The higher the frequency, the more the signals are deflected, reflected, or absorbed by the objects. The same considerations apply to determine the appropriate length for an antenna: The larger a fraction the length of an object is of the wavelength of an electromagnetic (radio) signal being directed at it, the more it tends to react to the signal in some way rather than just letting it pass. There are exceptions to this because of special properties of some materials, such as glass, but it holds true as a general rule. The appropriateness of using wireless communications in almost any situation is affected by this problem.

In fact, for the really high-frequency signals, such as light waves, which will be needed to carry the enormous amount of information characteristic in the future, there are a multitude of objects that interfere with communications over long distances, such as water droplets and dust particles. Hence the "wire" will come back into prominence for future telecommunications systems, but the wire itself will be a glass rod of hairlike width called an *optical fiber*. In a decade or two the optical fiber will supplant the familiar old pair of telephone wires as the preferred mode of telecommunications over city-sized distances. Because of the enormous bandwidth available in an optical signal it will be a simple matter to transmit all sorts of computer and other signals simultaneously down these broad telecommunications highways. In the meantime, evolutionary developments of current methods will occur.

Satellites

One way of getting around the problems of line-of-sight transmission for microwave signals is to look up—to a communications satellite. One of the most spectacularly useful products of the U.S. space program, communications satellites orbit in a plane that includes the earth's equator, at a distance of some 35,800 km (22,200 statute miles) from the surface of the earth. The reason this particular altitude is used is that a satellite rotating about the earth at that altitude makes exactly one rotation per day. Consequently, a satellite rotating in the same direction as the earth, from west to east, appears to remain fixed over a single point on the equator. In order to communicate with a communications satellite all you have to do is point your antenna to its location over the equator and talk, provided you have the proper antenna and equipment tied to it. Even so there can be a line-of-sight problem though: Communication satellites can see the earth's surface only between about 83 degrees north latitude and 83 degrees south latitude. This is not a problem unless you happen to be north of the northernmost tip of Greenland or in central Antarctica.

Communication satellites all require sophisticated transmission and reception equipment. However, as in the other areas of telecommunications and electronics, the costs are going down and the capabilities are going up. Direct broadcast satellites that send a signal directly to your home or office are just around the corner. As this is written it is possible to buy a home station, complete with "dish" antenna to receive commercial TV satellite transmissions. The possibilities for using the same sort of capabilities for computer data transmissions will be growing in coming years. The important point is that with satellite telecommunications, particularly with satellite-to-satellite signal relays, there are very few points on the surface of the earth that cannot be reached by telecommunications.

4

Thus far we have been considering mostly the technological events and trends that have been shaping the growing interest in telecommunications between microcomputers. But we must not lose sight of the fact that the most frequent reason for having microcomputers telecommunicate is to aid somehow in communication between humans and human institutions. Many of the new applications of microcomputers are "interactive": There is frequent interaction between the computer and one or more humans. The purposes vary widely, as we have seen and will explore further. But in all of them the computer must communicate meaningfully to the human and the human must communicate meaningfully to the computer. Lest we forget the human interface, this chapter will deal with some of the issues raised by human-machine communications.

THE WAYS PEOPLE COMMUNICATE

Most of us are accustomed to dealing with telecommunications systems, in particular with radios, TVs, and telephones. The only message we have for the machines of these basic telecommunications systems is that we desire their services, which we convey by turning them on or by picking up the telephone handset. There is no problem when the services are so simple.

With computers the situation is entirely different. We are not just talking through them, as we would through the telephone. We are not just listening to them and/or watching them, as we would the radio or TV. We are having fairly complicated conversations with them, almost as if we were communicating with another human being. If a computer system is designed so that communication with its human users is effective, the system will be much more readily accepted than one with which the communications are complex or difficult. The obtuse, intransigent-appearing system is likely to have a very short lifetime in a world where better alternatives are sprouting up daily. People will readily adapt to an easily used system. If it is particularly easy to use, they are likely to use it more than they had originally intended. Conversely, they will begin to ignore an uncommunicative system quickly, regardless of its other merits. In short, the more human-like the computer seems to be, the more readily it will be accepted and used by a variety of people.

Dialogues

This book addresses the topics of telecommunications and computers, so we are most concerned here with a dialogue process of one kind or another. We "talk"

Human-Computer Interactions

to the computer or, through the computer, to someone else or to another computer. The party on the other end of the telecommunications link responds to us. We answer, and so on.

One example of such a dialogue with a large, distant ("remote mainframe") computer is shown in Figure 4-1. The case shown in the figure is a simple one in which two tasks are performed after the user is "logged on" to the remote computer. First, the user, one "jdoe," asks the computer to display a directory of the files stored in the computer under the user's name. Second, the user asks the computer to list a program written in BASIC, via a text editor contained in the remote computer. The human inputs are underscored. After the program has been listed, the user quits the text editor and logs off the computer with a pair of single-letter commands. The computer responds with a signoff message including some statistics concerning the task just performed, preceded by the witty quotation of the hour.

This seems to be a rather pointless, albeit short, dialogue. However, in this case there is a dialogue within a dialogue. Only the inner dialogue is shown in Figure 4-1. The outer dialogue is between J. Doe and a personal computer. The personal computer takes care of the details of communicating with the remote computer, as we shall see in later chapters. J. Doe wants the maze-generating program that is stored in the remote computer to be sent to the personal computer so that it can be used independently of the big machine. Unfortunately, she does not remember the exact name of the maze program; hence the request to display the file directory. The personal computer telecommunications software has a provision for storing the information coming to it from the remote computer. So, when the program is listed by the text editor software on the remote machine, it is automatically saved by J. Doe's personal computer for later use.

Although this dialogue is straightforward, a simple conversation between the remote computer and J. Doe via a personal computer, it is not as simple as a conversation between two people. J. Doe needed some prior training before engaging in this dialogue. Portions of it are in a code that must be known by the user before an effective dialogue can take place.

The first of these coded interchanges occurs right at the start. The computer signifies that it is alive and ready to communicate by sending an "@" sign to the user. The "@" sign is known as a "prompt." It is an indication that the computer is ready to receive characters from the user. (Different computers use different prompts; a single computer may also change the prompt sign depending on the particular type of task it is performing.) When J. Doe saw the prompt

41

```
∂log jdoe zbqrg5 12345
Job 45 on TTY43 23-Oct 11:37:40

∂dir
   PS:<JDOE>
$XED-MOD..1
$XED-MODE-FILE$..5
ADDRESS.SAMP.3
AUTO-SAVE..4
CFRFINAL.81RPT.1,2
DCMODEM.Z80.1
EMACS.INIT.2
EVENT.CONSMSG.1
INFCTR.LPT.1,2
    .MSS.2,3,4,5,6
    .OTL.1,2
INFOCENTER.PROP.5,6
INST.TXT.6
JOBINI.MAC.1
LOGIN.CMD.4,5
MAIL.TXT.1
MAZE.BAS.1
PREDIS.OST.13
TECHNOLOGY.PARK.3

Total of 28 files
∂xed
:read
Input file: maze.bas.1 'Old generation!
184 lines
1:list
00003 INPUT H1$
00004 PAGE 66
00020 PRINT TAB(10);"USC PERSONAL COMPUTER ASSESSMENT PROJECT"
00030 PRINT TAB(10);"A DIFFERENT MAZE FOR EACH QUESTIONNAIRE"
00010 FOR I=1 TO 4
00012 PRINT
             .
             .
             .    [portion of text deleted in this illustration]

01092 FOR I=1 TO 66-(2*V+13)
01093 PRINT
01094 NEXT I
01100 END
:quit
∂z
A committee is a life form with six or more legs
   and no brain.
      - Lazarus Long

Killed Job 45, User JDOE Account 12345 TTY 43,
   at 23-Oct 11:41:12,  Used 0:00:02 in 0:03:35
```

Figure 4-1
Sample Computer Dialogue

she proceeded to log in (or on) to the computer by sending her name, a password (ordinarily not displayed but in this example, the zbqrg5 is shown), and an account number so that the computer knows whom to charge for the forthcoming events. A mistake in any one of those three character patterns would usually cause the computer to disconnect the user (by "hanging up" its telephone connection), although it might allow jdoe to try a few more times first.

Patterns

This sort of shorthand or codelike communication pattern is suitable for someone who has been trained in the use of the particular computer system at the other end of the communications link. It is much less attractive to the novice or even the expert but occasional user, neither of whom might know or remember the details of the codes for logging in or for causing other desired computer functions. People do not ordinarily speak to each other in code or in "shorttongue." They use entire sentences and phrases, replete with all the nouns, pronouns, conjunctions, and so forth, to ensure that their meaning is perceived by the other parties in the conversation. Furthermore, they do not change their vocabulary as they communicate with different people, unless of course the others are from different cultures. Things are different when a user is communicating with most contemporary computer systems, particularly at the communications interface.

People tend to communicate fairly well using the following kinds of rules:

1. There is much use of elaboration and redundancy. A person would say, "Please get me the file on George Jones," rather than, "Gt fil g.jones."

2. There is also much implicit meaning in a fairly short sentence. When asking for the file on George Jones, one does not have to say, "Go to the file cabinet that is third from the left of all the file cabinets. Look at the second drawer from the top. See if the label on the drawer says 'J'. If so, open the drawer. If not," and so on.

3. Sometimes words can be rearranged within a given utterance without much change in the meaning. "Yesterday I saw Judy," "I saw Judy yesterday," and "Judy? I saw her yesterday" all have much the same meaning to the human listener.

4. Conversationalists have memory. A dialogue starting out with, "Did you know that Herb was . . . ," and later containing, " . . . after that. Then he said . . ." would be unambiguous even if the subject of the conversation had changed. That is, one does not have to keep reminding the other person that the subject is Herb.

5. Ambiguity can be resolved by context. "When I got out the paint for the door, I found that it was red. So I had to go to the paint store after all." It seems that the paint was red, which was not the desired color for the door.

6. prcision in punkshewayshun kpITALisatin or speling is not rilly requyred for unnerstaning in most situations, even though errors may slow the communications process.

7. "Protocols" (ritual methods of behavior) are flexible. One does not need to open every conversation with "My name is X. What is your name?" Various forms of this greeting can be used, or it can be omitted, or it can be put elsewhere in the conversation.

8. Changes in emphasis can change meaning: "He would go there often" versus "He *would* go there often."

There are many other characteristics of so-called "natural" language like those just listed that serve to point out some of the problems of communicating with computers. Central to all of them is the notion of flexibility, the ability of humans to adapt to a variety of contexts and a number of modes of delivery and still maintain effective communication. Computers are not able to command this flexibility at their present stage of evolution.

Example

As an example of this present state of most interactive computer communications systems imagine the following telephone conversation between humans:

LOG-IN PROCEDURE

"Hello, Joe, whaddaya know?"

"Who is this?"

"It's me, Moe, Joe."

"I don't know any 'Moe, Joe.' Who is this?"

"It's Moe."

"Thank you. How do I know it's the real Moe?"

"Don't you recognize my voice?"

"I do not recognize voices. You have ten seconds to identify yourself properly or I'll hang up."

"OK, OK, my password is SHAZAM."

"Thank you, Moe. The meter is now running. Now, what can I do for you?"

TRANSACTIONS

"Give me a list of the games you have in your catalogue."

"I can't; you're not here."

"I mean, read me a list of the games in your catalogue."

"I can't; you're not here."

"I mean, read me a list of the games in your catalogue."

"Here is a list of the games I have in my catalogue: Adventure, Astrologer, Bingo, Blastoff, . . ." [Joe reads the list in a monotone.]

"OK, let me play the first one."

"Let you play the first what?"

"Let me play the first game."

"I have no file called 'the first game'."

Moe mutters to himself, then says, "Let me play Adventure."

"Adventure coming up. You are in a fearsome, foul forest. Around you are. . . . " The game goes on for a while, disturbed by frequent silences from Joe (as well as further evidences of dull wittedness), then Moe tires of it and tells Joe to quit playing. Joe replies.

"Now, what can I do for you?"

"Let's try another."

"I do not understand you."

"Let's try another game."

"Do you want a list of the games I have in my catalog?"

"I already have a list of your games. Let's try another."

"I do not understand you."

"I want to play another game."

"I have no file called 'another game'."

"Oh, forget it."

"I do not understand you."

Joe slams the phone down on the receiver.

HOW COMPUTERS RESPOND

In the past, computers have had much greater rigidity in their interactions with people than would be tolerated in communications among people. There are historical reasons for this. First, most communication with computers, until the mid-1960s, was in *batch* mode; the computer was fed a problem with a stack of punched cards, then left to its work. After the job was finished the results would be printed out for the user to decipher at leisure. There was no interactivity. All the possible uncertainties in the input information had to be figured out ahead of time; there was no way to change things in mid-compute. Therefore, programmers did not spend much time worrying about designing programs for effective interaction with humans—there just wasn't any!

As programs became more complex, with the growing power of the computers, it became more desirable to include some forms of interaction so that decisions about the next steps to be performed by the computers could be made along the way. Interpretive languages, such as BASIC, were invented that depended upon interaction with the programmer for effective program development. The concept of computer time-sharing grew increasingly popular, with many users sharing the same computer resources via telecommunications and remote terminals. But, alas, the batch-processing mode of communications interfacing still dominated. In many ways it still does.

The culprit primarily responsible for the impersonality, the unfriendliness, of computers as perceived by most people is the lack of attention on the part of hardware and software designers alike to the issues of the interface between people and computers. Computers generally have few of the attributes, listed earlier, which facilitate human-human communication. They are intolerant of entry errors, of departures from rigidly established communications protocols, of the use of synonyms or equivalent phrases. They often have to be told every detailed step they are to perform. They assume nothing, and they remember nothing about previous conversations or previous references in the same conversation. Consequently, they present a forbidding appearance indeed to the novice or infrequent computer user, not because of any fundamental limitation of computer physics, but because of a number of practical design tradeoffs (which led to the use of batch processing, but which are becoming less and less justifiable nowadays on the basis of relative costs). Many of these tradeoffs still influence design, of course, but they are losing their importance as the underlying technologies improve. Here are some of them.

SPEED. The first problem with the machine-person interface is speed. The earliest limiters of speed in a computer telecommunications environment were the terminals themselves. Until the late 1960s most telecommunications terminals were Teletype™ or similar printers, chugging along at about 15 characters per second, all in capital letters. That works out to about 150 words per minute, less than half as fast as many people read. The users of the computers wanted to get their information as fast as possible (typical victims of the "hurry" conditioning characteristic of Western civilization), so the greatest pressure was for abbreviating everything and using short codes instead of natural-language words and sentences. The limitations of the equipment made it worthwhile to train the users to decipher and use the codes.

The speed of contemporary computer-telecommunications equipment can be *much* greater, as we shall see later, but currently is twice as fast as it was then for most low-cost telecommunications systems. That is, a contemporary computer-telecommunications system will run at about 300 words per minute. Speeds can go higher than that under some, more costly, circumstances. A favorite higher-priced speed is 1200 words per minute. This is comfortable for speed readers and about as fast as is useful for many interactive tasks. As some of the impending technology becomes widely available, notably fiber optics and cable-based telecommunications, the problem of waiting for the telecommunications link to squeeze the information down its electronic pipe will largely disappear.

MEMORY. Memory space has always been a limiting factor in the design of computers. The most expensive physical part of a computer is usually its memory, if that is at all extensive. Therefore, back when software was cheap relative to hardware, the designer of a computer system was motivated to minimize the amount of memory used for such "extraneous" things as communicating with humans. After all, the argument went, if all the available memory is used up in communicating with the user, then there won't be any left to do the intended job, in which case why communicate at all?

The consequence of that line of reasoning is that the computer software is designed to allow communications only through an explicit, terse shorthand. There is no room for error. Frequently there is no room even for error *messages*. The inexperienced user either is cut off or finds weird things happening without explanation.

The dialogue in Figure 4-1 gives an indication of the possibilities for improving this situation. The computer at the end of the telecommunications link is a relatively large one, with several megabytes (million characters) of on-line fast memory. There is enough memory, even though the computer is serving many users simultaneously, so that some niceties can be included in the communications software to make it friendlier.

For example, while in the text-editing mode, entered by typing "xed" (for experimental editor in this case), the user need type only the first letter of a command. The computer fills in the rest to assure the user that the command was the intended one. If it was not the right command, the user is given a slightly better clue to what went wrong. A more typical situation, for the case of the system not well designed for the human interface, would be one in which those expansions are not supplied: Single-letter commands are used for almost everything; they are executed immediately; and no error or explanation messages are given—very unfriendly.

The cost of computer memory has been decreasing rapidly since the invention of the integrated circuit and, as explained earlier, it is likely to continue that decline for several more years. Nevertheless, the memory problem is likely to be with us for a while. What is low-cost memory to a corporation in the *Fortune 500* list is not necessarily low-cost to the average citizen who wishes to engage in some computer telecommunications. The dilemma remains: how much of the memory should be used in communicating in a human rather than a computer form?

HOUSEKEEPING. The previous two sets of issues are mostly hardware-related. There is one further problem with human-computer interaction in general that is usually compounded in computer-telecommunications systems in particular: housekeeping. That heading includes many different annoyances for the human user of a computer-telecommunications system. The reasons for the annoyance are two: the memory limitations already mentioned, and a series of software compromises generally lumped under the term "systems problems." These are the problems the computer has in keeping track of all the devices that are connected to it, including the operator's terminal and the "port" to which the outside communicator is connected.

In general, a computer that is in a telecommunications mode is also doing other things as well. In the case of relatively inexpensive microcomputers, sometimes these other things can take up a good deal of the computer's time. Not shown in the scene between Moe and Joe (the computer-like human) is that Joe kept suspending the game to attend to other things. That was because Joe had several telephones and was trying to engage in conversations on all of them at once. Many mainframe computers have had this problem for years. It is now becoming a problem of microcomputers as they engage in communications with several users, using a single CPU. The service to each user degrades as the number of users that has to be served increases.

The central problem here is that a single microprocessor is doing not only the calculations that are its forte, but also all the housekeeping chores: keeping track of who is connected to which port, what the topic of conversation is, what the charges (if any) for the time used should be, who has priority over whom when it comes to allocating time, where the information from each user should be stored, what . . . well, it can be a demanding job.

All of these housekeeping chores are under the control of the computer's "operating system." Much more will be said later about this piece of software. For now, what is important is that there are two basic types of operating system for telecommunications: single-user; and multi-user, or multi-tasking. At the low-cost end of the microcomputer spectrum, there are, as you might expect, only single-user operating systems. It is obviously a much more complicated job to handle several users simultaneously (or apparently simultaneously) than it is to deal with a single user. And, of course, the more complicated operating system uses more memory, although the space required by an operating system is not proportional to the number of users it can handle.

The other aspect of housekeeping that is important is also software-related. That is the ability of the interface software to behave flexibly. As we saw from the scenario and the example of a real transaction, most computer systems are relatively inflexible in the ways they will accept input and/or provide responses. If the operating system is to be able to respond to a variety of possible inputs that are to result in the same end operation of the microcomputer, then the possible inputs must somehow be stored in or accessible to the system at all times. Again, the result is an increased demand for fast memory and an effective system for associating these variable inputs with the proper computer responses. As research in artificial intelligence over the past few years has shown, that task is far more easily specified than done. The more one explores the complexity of the processes required in even relatively simple forms of intercomputer communications, the more one begins to appreciate the effectiveness of the human brain in coping effortlessly with all these details.

PROBLEMS FOR THE SYSTEM DESIGNER

All of the preceding material is background for one of the basic themes that underlies the rest of this book: ultimately, the basic purpose of computer-telecommunications systems is to facilitate communications among humans. If the systems are to be successful they must be designed with this goal as one of the foremost ones. This priority does not necessarily create great hardships for the system designer, provided some of the niceties needed for friendly communications with humans are thought of and allowed for *as the system is being built*. For the reader who is simply interested in getting a personal computer to communicate with others any way it can, the problems covered in this chapter may not be significant—until the reader has to train someone else to use the system quickly. For the reader interested in producing a system that will be readily accepted by novice computer users it is important to keep in mind that the interface with the users has to *appear* simple, even if it takes greater complexity in the computer or the software itself.

It is also a great advantage if the design of the telecommunications system, including its operating software, can be kept as straightforward as possible. This seems to be a philosophy of design that is often stated and at least as often ignored. The basic reason for this philosophy is that systems always seem to change after they have been "firmly and unalterably" specified. Hence it is necessary for the long-term mental health of the system designer that the design be readily interpretable and comprehensible when the designer comes back six months later to fine-tune it, add capabilities, or fix those errors that had supposedly been worked out earlier.

This also means that the system should be well documented at every level, from the assembly-language routines required to run pieces of the hardware all the way up to the manual that gently leads the novice user into a state of confident expertise in the use of the system. That millenium is not yet here. However astounding the technological advances of microelectronics may be, much of the burden of translating human thoughts into symbols which the machines understand, and vice versa, will still rest with the user and with the system designer.

The following chapters will deal with the practical aspects of applying some of these philosophical concepts. Because of the rate of change of the technology, both in hardware and in software, it is not possible to cover all the details of each system or communications component available at the moment when this book is being read. Many of the components discussed later are now, or will be, integrated into systems in such a way that they are not explicity seen by the user. They are there nevertheless, in some form or other. I hope that, through reading the next few chapters and trying some of the concepts presented, the reader will be able to understand the basic concepts of computer telecommunications and to develop an effective system suited to his or her needs.

PRACTICAL EXAMPLES

ow that we have reviewed some of the reasons for the growing interest
in computer communications, some history, and some ideas for further
growth, it is time to discuss how computer communications are accomplished.
There are a few principles of practical data communications which apply no
matter the details of the communication system used. The purpose of this chapter
and the next few is to cover those principles in the context of commercially
available technological options, and so we will concentrate on the most common
method of data communications for the individual computer owner: the modem
telephone link to other computers.

KEY COMPONENTS OF
THE COMMUNICATION SYSTEM

Much of the complexity and expense in the hardware for microcomputer communications is necessitated by the fact that we communicate over telephone
lines. We don't always have to communicate that way. We could arrange it so
that our computers talked to other computers of the same kind as ours only over
"hard wired" connections. This situation is shown in Figure 5-1. If both computers were identical in their hardware and software capabilities, and if their
operating systems would permit it (more on that later), then Computer A could
treat Computer B as a simple extension of itself and vice versa. This is the
situation that exists in a simple "local network." A local network is a collection
of computers and peripheral equipment connected by a hard-wired communication network independent of the telephone system. The term "hard wired"
means that there are physical wires permanently connected between the components in the system.

Having mentioned the existence of local networks, I am going to defer the
discussion of their details until Chapter 9, because most applications for local

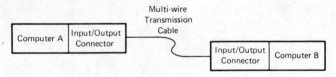

Figure 5-1
A Simple Intercomputer Connection

Hardware Necessary
for Communications

networks are in multi-user office or production-line environments. I will first develop some basic information about the details of simpler communications systems. Most practical local-network setups use many of the data-manipulation techniques described here. In any case, most individual microcomputer owners are mainly concerned about developing communications with other computers located at a distance, and often of a type different from their own. For this application the telephone system is the best available means of communication.

There are two essential features of the telephone system that are of interest to us. The first is that it is so convenient: it can allow us to get in contact with others almost anywhere on the surface of the earth—even if it has to go through outer space to do it. The second feature is the reason we need modems (the topic of most of the rest of this book): the telephone system was designed and optimized for the communication of voices, not of digital signals. This situation is changing; in the future it will be much easier to transmit digital signals directly over the telephone system. In the meanwhile, the modem is a requirement.

Modems—An Introduction

The name MODEM is an acronym for MOdulator/DEModulator. A modem is an electronic system which translates the analog signals with which the telephone system is comfortable into digital signals with which the computer is comfortable, and vice versa. The process of converting digital signals into analog signals, in forms acceptable to the telephone system, is called modulation. The process of converting analog signals into digital signals is called demodulation. The modem does both.

PARALLEL—SERIAL DATA CONVERSION. The digital signals of interest to us are those produced by our microcomputers and the computers with which they are to communicate. The design of contemporary computers gives us our first problem. The information running around inside our computers is almost universally transmitted in "parallel" form. That is, each bit position in a digital "word" sent from one component to another in the computer has its own signal path (its own wire), so that information can be transmitted a word rather than a bit at a time. The parallel mode of transmission was assumed for the simple two-computer network of Figure 5-1. In eight-bit computers there are at least eight wires reserved for data transmission. Usually there are sixteen wires: eight for sending information, and eight for receiving it. In sixteen-bit computers there are usually sixteen (less often thirty-two) internal wires for data transmission, and so on. Figure 5-2a shows an 8-wire cable system for sending data from Computer A to Computer B.

The telephone line you are most likely to encounter has only two wires. One way to cope with this problem in the case of computer communication might be to pick a pair of the wires in the computer's internal communications bus and send just the information appearing on those two wires. This is analogous to dividing each printed line in this book into eight or sixteen horizontal linelets, as a dot-matrix printer does, then transmitting just two of those linelets. The results might constitute a form of modern art but would not be likely to convey much information. A large fraction of the information would be missing.

A better technique for preserving the information content of the digital signal is to convert it from parallel into serial form. This conversion is shown in Figure 5-2b. The binary word to be transmitted is changed from a set of 0s and 1s appearing simultaneously at eight wires to a sequence of 0s and 1s travelling in order on a single wire. This conversion allows the use of fewer wires, but requires more time. Instead of sending all eight bits at once we must send them sequentially; furthermore we must now add information to the signal, in the form of extra bits, so that the computer at the other end of the transmission line can know where one "word" ends and the next begins. Thus it can take ten times

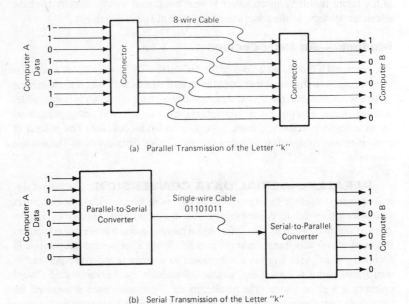

(a)   Parallel Transmission of the Letter "k"

(b)   Serial Transmission of the Letter "k"

Figure 5-2
Serial vs. Parallel Transmission

as long, or more, to send a set of eight bits in serial form, as it does to send the same word in parallel form. From now on I will confine the discussion to eight-bit computers. The same principles apply to 4-, 12-, 16-, 24-, and 32-bit computers, although the details of data transmission with some of these other systems may become slightly more complicated.

The first task of a computer communication system, when it is sending a digital signal, is to convert the signal from parallel to serial form. The next task is to add extra bits to each byte so that it can be separated from previous and subsequent bytes. It may also add a bit to be used for checking the accuracy of the transmission. Finally, the system must include a modem to convert the digital data to analog signals which can be transmitted over the telephone and which can be demodulated by other modems to reconstitute the original digital signal.

BIDIRECTIONALITY. Another key function of the modem is to allow data to be transmitted in both directions simultaneously. Figures 5-3 and 5-4 illustrate the situation. As you probably know, most telephones have only two wires connecting them to the telephone network, as Figure 5-3 shows. In this case, when both parties speak simultaneously, both signals appear on the line at once. This does not present a problem if the length of wire between the two telephones is short; the signal from telephone A is loud enough to be heard adequately at telephone B, and vice versa. Furthermore, the human conversationalists can usually understand each other even if they occasionally speak simultaneously.

If the distance between telephones is so long that the signal from A to B, or from B to A, is greatly reduced by the resistance of the wires, then the signals must be amplified. Amplifiers are unidirectional devices: a signal coming into one side of the amplifier is amplified and sent out the other side, but a signal coming in the other side does not come out at all. The difficulty in our two-wire telephone system, then, is that an amplifier can increase the loudness of only one of the signals, say from A to B. B's signal, if also reduced by distance, will not be loud enough to reach A. The most obvious way to solve this problem is to expand to a four-wire system, as shown in Figure 5-4.

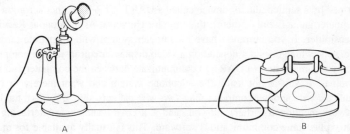

A

B

Figure 5-3
A Two-wire Telephone Connection

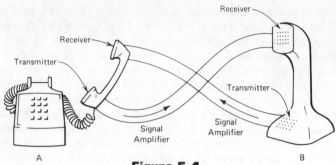

Figure 5-4
A Four-wire Telephone Connection

In a four-wire system each signal path has its own amplifier. Many private telephone systems are of the four-wire variety. Another advantage is that there is no possibility that the signal from A to B will interfere with the signal from B to A. A disadvantage is that the system uses twice as much wire (or its equivalent). In practice the telephone system uses two-wire lines for its local distribution of signals, and four-wire lines for long-distance transmission or whenever else amplifiers are needed; the transition from one system to the other is accomplished at the local switching center by a device called a hybrid coil. In any case, the modem must be capable of coping with the extra requirements placed on the system by this requirement for bidirectionality. Before we look further at the modem, let us examine the device that performs the task of getting the computer signal ready for transmission or reception.

The UART

Figure 5-5 diagrams the main components of an "asynchronous" communications unit in terms of the function just described. It is called asynchronous because the signals between the communicating units can arrive at random times, not subject to the control of some master clock. In microcomputer communications systems the task of converting between parallel and serial data is usually performed by a semiconductor device called a UART. This is another acronym (the computer game is full of them), this time for Universal Asynchronous Receiver/ Transmitter. If you currently have a computer system with a separate terminal (i.e., one which does not depend on a video display circuit inside the computer) then you already have a UART to communicate between the computer and your terminal. If you're not using the telephone system and want merely to communicate with another computer via a two-wire cable (a simple form of the local network mentioned earlier), all you need is a UART and some interfacing circuitry plus some communications software. This is usually available for microcomputers in the form of a serial interface board which plugs right into your machine. This component is enclosed in dashed lines in Figure 5-5.

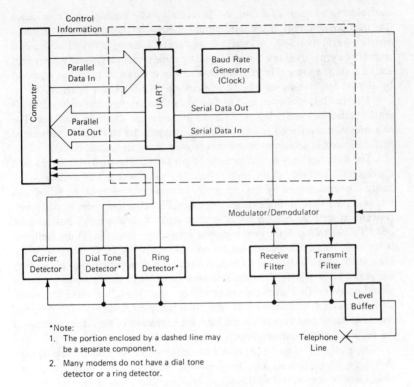

Figure 5-5
An Asynchronous Communication Unit

The UART also takes care of the job of adding the extra bits to each byte to be transmitted. Finally, it sets up the timing for transmission of the signal so that it goes out at the proper, or at least at the selected, "baud rate." The baud rate, for our purposes, is the transmission rate in bits per second at which each byte (and its attached extra bits) is transmitted. Even though characters (bytes, for the moment) are transmitted and received asynchronously (i.e., at random intervals) by the UART, within each character the bits must be transmitted and received at a fixed rate. Otherwise the UART becomes hopelessly confused.

A Technical Digression: In case *you* are hopelessly confused at this point, let us go step by step through the process of transmitting a byte to another computer.

Signalling Format: At both ends of the communication line the computers are normally in what is known as an idle state between the transmission/reception of characters. In the idle state a continuous voltage is transmitted, equivalent to a logical *1*, or "mark." This is a fail-safe mechanism; a continuous 0 is thus possible only if the transmitting computer "crashes," that is, is inoperative (see Figure 5-6). A logical *0*, or "space," lasting a large fraction of a second or more is used as a "break" signal by some computer systems for interrupt and/or reset purposes. The transmission of a new character is always signalled by a "start bit," which must be an interruption of the voltage, hence a *0*.

The start bit is followed by 5 to 8 data bits. The exact number of bits depends on the particular code being used for the transmission—more on that later. The sequence of transmission is such that the least significant bit (LSB) is transmitted first, followed in sequence by the successively more significant bits.

The data bits may be followed by a parity bit. The parity bit serves as a check on the accuracy of the transmission. Its value is 0 or 1 depending on the parity convention used by the computers and on the content of the set of data bits being transmitted. For example, if a signal is being sent under an odd parity convention then the number of *1*s in each set of data-plus-parity bits must be odd. If *11001011* is being sent with odd parity, then the value of the parity bit is set to *0*, because the data contains an odd number of *1*s. Conversely, if the same data, *11001011*, were to be sent under the even-parity convention, then the parity bit would be *1* so that the number of *1*s in the data-plus-parity set would be even. Two other parity conventions are "mark," in which the parity bit is always a *1*, and "space," in which the parity bit is always a *0*. Of course these two latter conventions do not have the advantage of providing a check on the accuracy of the transmission.

The parity bit, if any, is followed by one or more "stop bits." Stop bits are always *1*s. Three options have been used in the past: 1, 1.5, and 2 stop bits. Most UARTs only have two options: 1 or 2 stop bits. This is because the 1.5-bit (in terms of the UART's clock) convention is used only for low-speed teletype-like systems, which generally use electromechanical methods for signal generation and reception. In any case, the number selected depends on the particular transmission protocol being used.

Finally, the system returns to the idle or mark state until the next character is to be transmitted.

The function of the UART is to arrange all these details, in cooperation with the computer and the modem. Here is how it is done (see Figure 5-7).

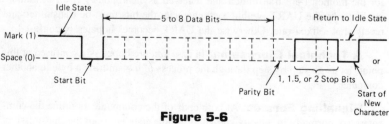

Figure 5-6
Data Formatting

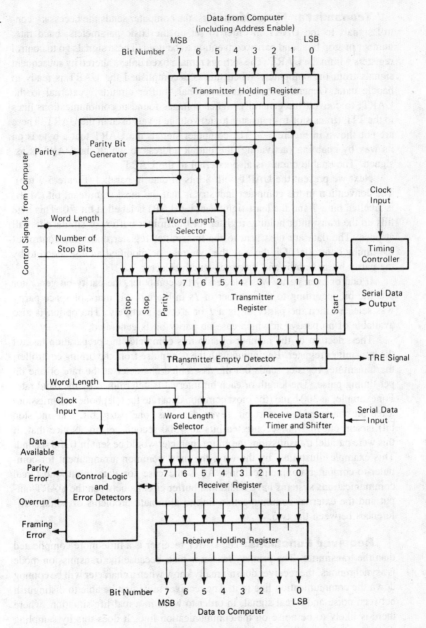

**Figure 5-7
UART Block Diagram**

Transmitter Functions: First the computer sends the necessary control signals to the UART in order to set up the basic parameters: baud rate, number of stop bits, and parity convention to be used. These signals go to control registers within the UART. The settings remain fixed unless altered by subsequent signals from the computer. When this is accomplished the UART is ready to handle data. Generally there are additional "buffer circuits," external to the UART, to convert the generally higher voltages found in communications lines to the TTL (transistor-to-transistor logic) voltage levels used in the UART. These are not shown in Figure 5-7. The computer signals the UART that a byte is on its way by enabling (activating) the output address to which the UART is assigned. The enable circuit is also external to the UART.

Next we present the UART with 8 bits of data in parallel (Figure 5-7 top). The convention in the computer industry is that the most significant bit (MSB) is labelled bit #7 and the least significant bit (LSB) is labelled bit #0. This byte fills up the transmitter holding register (or transmitter buffer, or similar title) all at once. The data are next sent to the transmitter register under the control of the timing controller. On the way the byte may be modified and/or added to by the parity-bit generator and the word-length selector.

If odd or even parity was selected by the computer, the parity-bit generator sets the bit according to the number of *1*s in the byte. If mark or space parity was selected then the parity bit is a *1* or a *0,* respectively. The option is also available of no parity, in which case no parity bit is generated.

The selection of the number of stop bits completes the preparation task of the transmitter register. Beginning with the next pulse from the timing controller, the transmitter register sends out the assembled character at the rate of one bit per timing pulse. The length of each bit interval is determined by the baud rate. For example, at 300 baud (the most common data rate for telephone transmission) a ten-bit character (one start bit, seven data bits, one parity bit, and one stop bit) is sent out in 1/30 second: ten bits at 1/300 second per bit. Notice that, if this were parallel transmission, the entire character would be sent in 1/300 second. This example illustrates, by the way, the most common arrangement for computer-to-computer communications. As is the case for data input, most real communications systems have additional buffer circuits between the UART output and the external communication link to eliminate problems of voltage differences between the two.

Receiver Functions: The UART receiver is a little more complicated than the transmitter. The primary reason is that, because the transmission mode is asynchronous, the receiver doesn't really know when a character will be coming down the communication line to it. The receiver must first be able to distinguish between noise and a real signal, in order to work in a real-life situation, where there is likely to be noise on the communication line. It does this by sampling the communication-line interface at a rate 16 times the rate at which it expects bits to be coming in. Thus for a transmission rate of 300 bits per second the

UART receiver would sample the line 4800 times per second. When the receiver detects a *0* (space) it starts a counter that counts the next eight sampling intervals (i.e., the next eight 4800-hundredths of a second, or half a bit interval). The receiver then checks again to see if the line is at *0*. If so, it assumes that the incoming signal really is a signal, not noise, and continues with the rest of the decoding process. The theory behind this is that it is relatively unlikely (though of course not impossible) that noise pulses would cause *0*s at precisely the start and midpoint of a bit interval.

Much of the rest of the receiving process is the reverse of the transmitting process. The receiver's data timer and shifter shift the incoming bits, one by one, into the receiver register. During this process the incoming word is checked for length and parity. An error signal is generated if the incoming character is not of the parity the receiver has been set to expect. During the length check the character is tested to make sure the last bit (or bits) is a (are) 1. If not, a "framing error signal" is generated to indicate that something is amiss with the incoming character. In a well regulated system, framing errors are relatively rare. The most likely cause of a framing error is that the receiver and the transmitter at the other end of the communication line are operating at different baud rates. For example, if the receiver were expecting an incoming signal at 600 baud and the actual signal were to be at 300 baud, the receiver would count the first five incoming bits as ten—it would not attach any significance to the fact that the data seemed to be coming always in pairs. At some point in the data stream the tenth bit would be a *0* (assuming the ten-bit code used earlier) and the receiver would signal a framing error.

Another type of error exists: an "overrun error." This is caused by the next character's coming in before the receiver has had a chance to send the last one to the computer. The possibility of an overrun error is diminished by the facts that the data are transferred to the computer in parallel, probably in a fraction of a receiver bit period, and that each character is sent to a "holding register" as soon as it is detected as complete in the receiver register.

At typical telephone communication rates, 150 to 1200 baud, overrun errors are rare. Most microcomputers can easily keep up with such rates as long as they are operating in a single-tasking mode (are not trying to do other things beside telecommunicate) and are not using an excessively inefficient modem control program. Consequently, many microcomputer systems ignore the overrun signal from the UART. However, at higher data rates, such as are found in direct-wired or local-network telecommunications, the assumption that the computer can keep up with the communications without checking for overflow may be dangerous. In any case, errors or no, a *data available signal* is generated to tell the computer that a character is ready for it to read.

By the way, if the computer is not paying attention and ignores the data available flag the UART will keep right on receiving characters and transferring them to the receiver holding register, sending its overrun signal the while. The result may be a substantial quantity of lost data. The computer communications system designer must take this possibility into account before deciding to ignore such error signals on the basis that they are unlikely to occur under the circumstances for which the system was designed. Systems are often used under circumstances for which they were not designed.

Before we leave the discussion of the UART it is important to recognize that the UART, with some buffer circuits, suffices as the interface for a simple communication system. Most commercially available serial I/O boards for microcomputers contain one or more UARTs, each of which has an RS-232 interface connector associated with it. The term RS-232 refers to a specification of the Electronic Industries Association (EIA) regarding the electrical characteristics of telecommunications signals. This will be discussed in more detail later in this chapter.

Two computers can be connected together with such a simple interface. Data can be transferred between computers in this manner, just as data are transferred between the individual computers and their peripherals, such as disk drives, printers and display consoles. In fact, for many microcomputer systems, the printer is a serial device which communicates with the computer via a UART and a set of RS-232 interface connectors. No modem is required for these situations.

More About Modems

As mentioned earlier, the purpose of the modem is to translate the digital signals which computers use into a form compatible with the telephone system. Specifically, the modem converts digital 1s and 0s to tones at specified frequencies, a pair for signal transmission and a pair for signal reception. In this way the modem converts the pair of telephone wires over which the signal is sent into the equivalent of two separate circuits and achieves the bidirectionality discussed earlier.

Figure 5-8 shows the typical frequency response of the switched telephone network. The nominal limits of response of the telephone system are 300 Hz and 3000 Hz. These are the frequencies at which the transmitted power is half that of the main portion of the response spectrum. This entire spectrum is not available for modem signaling and data transmission; a signal at 2600 Hz, for example, would cause the phone line to be disconnected by the automatic equipment at the telephone switching center. Eight other tones are used by the touch tone dialing system (at 697 Hz, 770 Hz, 852 Hz, 941 Hz, 1209 Hz, 1336 Hz, 1447 Hz, and 1633 Hz). Of course, automatic dialing devices may use these frequencies—more on that later. For data transmission, however, the modem must pick other working frequencies to avoid interference. The actual frequencies used vary with the signalling rate of the modem; one set is used at rates up to 600 baud, others at rates between 600 and 1200 baud.

Modems operate in two modes: *originate* and *answer*. The lowest-cost modems operate in the originate mode only. This is because they are designed to be used with "dumb" terminals in the traditional time-sharing service. This is called the originate mode because the interchange between the modem-terminal and the remote computer is originated at the modem end of the telecommunications link. Similarly, if the microcomputer to which the modem is connected is to be used only as a means of communicating with another computer at the behest of the microcomputer operator, then an originate-only modem should be adequate. If, on the other hand, the microcomputer is to be used only to receive information from external data sources, then an answer-only modem would satisfy the communications requirements. If the microcomputer in question is to be capable both of originating transmissions to another computer and of receiving calls from another computer, then a modem capable of performing both functions—an originate/answer modem—is required.

The difference between the two modes of operation lies only in the frequencies used by the modem. The *de facto* standards for data communications in the United States have been established by AT&T. There are several different sets of frequencies in widespread use for the switched telephone network. One set is the standard baud rates up to 600. There are at least three sets of frequencies used for baud rates up to 1200, and some modems are becoming available which will operate up to 1200 baud using the frequencies of the 0-to-600-baud set. However, we will confine our attention, for the moment, to the so-called low-speed (transmission rates up to 600 baud) asynchronous scheme of operations.

LOW-SPEED ASYNCHRONOUS MODEMS. In the originate mode the modem transmits *0*s (or spaces) at 1070 Hertz and *1*s (or marks) at 1270 Hertz. That is, when the UART sends a *0* to the modem, the modem sends a 1070 Hertz tone to the telephone line. The duration of the tone is the reciprocal of the baud rate (or some integer multiple of it for successive *0*s). For example, if the baud rate is 300 the *shortest* tone the modem will send lasts 1/300 of a second, or 3.333 milliseconds. A similar sequence occurs for transmission of *1*s. When the originate mode modem *receives* an incoming signal at 2025 Hertz or at 2225 Hertz it signals the detection of a *0* or a *1*, respectively.

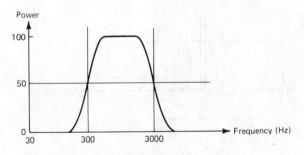

Figure 5-8
Telephone Network Frequency Response

In the answer mode the process is the same, except that the two pairs of frequencies are reversed. The answer-mode modem transmits at 2025 and 2225 Hertz and receives at 1070 and 1270 Hertz. These arrangements are shown in Figure 5-9. These particular frequency arrangements and modes of operation are those used by the Bell Type 103 series of modems. Modems of the 103 type need not be manufactured by Western Electric (the manufacturing arm of AT&T); many manufacturers now produce 103-compatible equipment.

Just to complicate matters, however, the 103-type frequencies are not internationally standardized. In fact, there is an international standard, promulgated by the Comité Consultatif International Telephonique et Telegraphique (CCITT), an arm of the United Nations, which sets an entirely different frequency pattern. Under the CCITT recommendations (they are not binding standards on all the UN nations), originate modems transmit 0s at 980 Hertz and 1s at 1180 Hertz, and receive 0s at 1850 Hertz and 1s at 1650 Hertz. This lack of real standardization is not a problem for the microprocessor-system builder who is concerned only about operating the system solely in the U.S. or, for example, solely in West Germany, because most computer-communications systems in the U.S. use the Bell Type 103 frequencies at low baud rates, and most West German systems use the CCITT frequencies. The trouble begins when the international traveller tries to use a U.S. system in West Germany, or vice versa.

DUPLEX MODES. The next issue to be faced in the design or assembly of a computer-telecommunications system is that of the manner in which the two computers communicate with each other. The simplest system uses the "simplex" mode, in which the originate-only computer/modem or terminal sends its signal to the intended recipient with no possibility of getting a signal back; that is, the transmission is one-way. This is clearly not a desirable mode for cases where interactive communications are required.

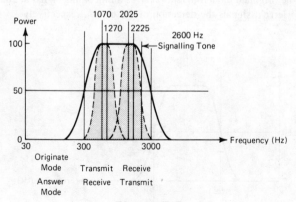

Figure 5-9
Low-Speed Modem Frequencies

More common for asynchronous data transmission are the two "duplex" modes: *full-duplex* and *half-duplex*. In full-duplex communication the computers at both ends of the communication link are free to transmit data at any time; one computer can transmit data while the other is also transmitting. In half-duplex transmission only one computer can transmit at a time, not both simultaneously as in full-duplex. In hard-wired systems the use of full duplex without a modem requires that there be separate transmit and receive lines between the communicating systems. Because the modem provides the equivalent of separate wires by virtue of its two sets of communication frequencies it is inherently capable of full-duplex transmission.

Full-duplex transmission should not, however, always be used by a modem, simply because it is available. In many cases, such as communication with most IBM computers, half-duplex transmission, is more desirable, primarily for operator reassurance. For example, if a microcomputer system is transmitting data to another computer using full-duplex, the other computer typically *echos* the data to the sender, providing assurance that the information was received as sent or, by virtue of discrepancies between the transmitted and echoed data, notification that there are errors in transmission. This means of operation is also called "echo-plex." If the transmission is half-duplex the receiving computer does not echo the data. If the microcomputer transmitting the information does not have a means of self-echoing the data the operator may be uncertain whether the transmission is even occurring or, at least, which data the computer is transmitting at the moment.

BASIC ELEMENTS OF THE MODEM. The basic elements of the modem are the modulator/demodulator, the buffer circuits, the carrier detector, and the ring and dial-tone connectors.

Modulator/demodulator: The lower section of Figure 5-5 shows the basic elements of a low speed asynchronous full-duplex modem. The key element of a modem is the modulator/demodulator. This is usually a single chip in contemporary modems. The purpose of the modulator/demodulator is to convert the serial data from the UART into digitally synthesized sine-waves at the appropriate frequencies, and to convert incoming sine-waves into their appropriate digital-data counterparts. Actually, the incoming sine wave is usually converted into a square wave before being sent to the modulator/demodulator. The specific frequencies used depend on whether the modem is in the originate or the answer mode; a control signal from the computer to the modulator/demodulator chip makes the selection. Alternatively, the modulator/demodulator may be permanently wired in one mode or may be switch-selectable.

Buffer Circuits: Generally the "sine wave" produced by the modulator/demodulator chip is very noisy, containing a number of frequencies other than the pure tone desired by the telephone network. This is because it really starts out in life as a "square" wave, whose rough edges must be removed before it is presentable. Hence the signal must be passed through a transmit filter before it is sent. To further ensure that the signal produced by the modem doesn't interfere with the telephone network there may be some level-buffering circuits as well before the signal finally gets to the telephone line. The buffering circuits establish the proper output voltage level and impedance for telephone-line compatibility. Some of the early modems designed for microcomputers did not have the output buffer circuits or, equally important, did not have circuits approved by the FCC. In those cases an additional set of buffer circuits, called a "data access arrangement" (DAA) is required to ensure compatibility with the telephone system. Received signals go through the inverse of the transmit process: they pass through a level buffer and a receive filter (to separate other telephone signals from the desired ones), and possibly through an amplifier-limiter which converts the filtered sine waves into squarish waves before presentation to the modulator/demodulator.

Carrier Detector: All commercial originate-only or originate/answer modems also have a carrier detector. The carrier detector looks for a signal at 2225 Hz. If it doesn't detect one for a period ranging from 100 milliseconds to 2 or more seconds, depending on the particular manufacturer or on the software in the modem controller, it generates a signal to the computer that the carrier is lost. For modems external to the computer the "signal" may be a light or a light-emitting diode (LED).

There are two reasons that the carrier detector uses 2225 Hz as its reference. First, a modem in the answer mode that is not transmitting data sends a continuous mark of 1 on its transmit line, as we saw earlier, at 2225 Hz. Even if the answer modem is transmitting data to an originate-mode modem it is unlikely that it will be transmitting only spaces for more than 100 or 200 milliseconds (the typical duration of a "break" signal). Therefore, the absence of the mark signal for a longer period is a good indication that there is nothing going on at the other end of the line.

Second, the 2225-Hz carrier serves a useful purpose for data transmissions over long distances. One of the characteristics of the human-conversation-oriented telephone system is that a voice transmission is echoed from the other end of the line. This provides a reassuring feedback to the converser. The trouble arises when the telephone connection between two conversationalists becomes too long, greater than about 1700 miles. Then the echo arrives at a time so much later than the time at which the sound was originated that it causes confusion to the speaker. To solve this problem devices called echo-suppressors are used. Echo-suppressors detect which of the two conversants is talking the louder and allow only that signal to go from its origin to its destination. The weaker *echo,* travelling in the other direction, is suppressed. The conversation is much clearer. If you have talked over a long-distance connection on which the echo-suppressor was not working you know the effect. While this fix is fine for people, it does not work for full-duplex data transmission, in which it is desirable to have signals going both ways simultaneously. The filters in the modems would take care of the echo problems, because the transmit frequencies of a modem are ignored by its receiver circuits. No additional "help" is needed from echo-suppressors.

Fortunately, the echo-suppressors can be turned off. They will cease to function if they receive a single-frequency tone, at a level close to the maximum level of the transmission, somewhere within the frequency band of 2010 to 2240 Hz, lasing at least 400 milliseconds. They will continue to stay off the line if there are no further interruptions of greater than 100 milliseconds in the signal being transmitted. The normal operation of the modem in the answer mode fulfills these requirements.

Ring and Dial-Tone Detectors: Some modem packages also have dial-tone and ring detectors. These are the packages which also perform automatic answering or dialing. The ring detector is used by the modem when it is in the answer mode. The purpose of the ring detector, as its name implies, is to discover when the modem is being called. A typical telephone jack, such as a modular connector, has four wires, only two of which are generally of interest to us. These are the "tip" and the "ring" wires, so named because they correspond to the tip and adjacent ring conductors in the original switchboard telephone systems (see Figure 3-2c). In any case, during idle periods, when the telephone is not in use, there is a potential difference of about 50 volts DC between these two wires. When the telephone rings, an AC signal of about 90 volts is superimposed on the 50V DC. The frequency of the AC ringing signal is between 15 and 70 Hz. Each ring lasts about 1 second. The ring detector senses this signal and sends a ring-detect signal to the computer.

The dial-tone indicator is used when the modem is in the originate mode. In some autodialers the presence of a dial tone is detected by a relatively so-phisticated circuit which senses the change from direct ground to resistance ground when the telephone exchange activates the dial tone. This arrangement requires an addition to the regular telephone line, called a "ground start." Other dial-tone indicators simply use an audio filter. If a signal is detected shortly after the dialer connects to the telephone line (goes "off hook") the dialer assumes that it is a dial tone. Many autodialing modems operate on the assumption that a dial tone will exist after a certain length of time and proceed accordingly, without actually listening. These systems do not have dial-tone detectors—more on that when we get to a discussion of software.

The purpose of the dial-tone indicator is quite straightforward: it is to prevent the modem/autodialer from starting to dial before the telephone system is ready (the line to the exchange is connected). The ring detector, on the other hand, has some uses other than simply sensing that a call is being attempted. One important function is to alert the computer to look for a signal at 1070 and/or 1270 Hz when the modem is connected to the line. If no such signal is detected after the modem is taken off hook, then the chances are that the incoming call is a voice rather than a data call. The computer must then decide what to do next, such as hang up.

The ring detector is very important in cases where the computer is the "host" of a time-sharing service. If there is a momentary loss of the carrier, followed by the carrier's reappearance, it is very important to know whether the loss of carrier was due to signal problems or to the termination of one call followed by the appearance of a new call. In the latter case, the previous caller's files on the computer must be secured before the new caller is attended to. Otherwise the new caller may be improperly connected to the previous caller's files. If there is no ring detector this occurrence can be all too common. The ring detector eliminates this problem through the computer software. If the reappearance of the carrier after the momentary loss is accompanied by a ring signal, then it is a new caller; if there is no ring signal then the old caller is still connected.

HIGHER-SPEED ASYNCHRONOUS MODEMS. Most of the lower-cost modems available for microcomputers are low-speed asynchronous modems. Data rates of 300 baud are acceptable for many users. However, the interest in higher data rates is generally awakened in a microcomputer user shortly after he or she encounters the first extended interactive session with another computer, or begins to transfer large files between computers. Usually the next step up from a low-speed modem is to a modem running asynchronously at 1200 baud. This factor of four in data transfer speed can have substantial effects on the user's boredom coefficient, as well as the size of the check to the telephone company.

Most low-speed modems in the U.S. are of the Bell 103-type; many 1200-baud modems are of the Bell 202- or 212-type. The 202-type modem uses a set of frequencies different from those the 103-type uses, and operates only in half-duplex. Its frequency pattern is shown in Figure 5-10. Only two data frequencies are used: 1200 Hz to represent a mark or *1*, and 2200 Hz to represent a space or *0*. The receiving modem may also transmit a signal at 387 Hz to tell the transmitting modem that the receiver is still on the line, or perhaps to indicate an error in transmission. As in the case of low-speed modems, the Bell frequencies and the CCITT-recommended frequencies are different; CCITT uses 1300 Hz for a mark and 2100 Hz for a space. Typically, 1200-baud modems in the late 1970s cost 3 to 4 times as much as type-103 modems. Now, as more sophisticated modem chips are appearing, 1200-baud modems are rapidly decreasing in price.

As microelectronic components take on an increasing number of sophisticated functions, the costs of modems will decrease and their functionality will increase. One of the techniques used to increase data rates for synchronous communications systems is "phase modulation." Figure 5-11 shows examples of phase modulation and of the frequency-shift modulation that has been the subject of our discussion up to now.

As the title implies, frequency-shift modulation, or frequency-shift keying

(FSK), as it is called in the communications field, refers simply to the use of different frequencies to represent *1*s and *0*s. In phase-shift keying (PSK), a single *carrier* frequency is used. This frequency is shifted in phase in such a manner as to represent the desired information. For example, a phase angle of 0 degrees might represent a *0*, a phase of angle of 180 degrees a *1*, as shown in Figure 5-9c. This is called coherent phase-shift keying because the "coherence," that is, the stability, of the carrier signal must be maintained so that it is clear which signal is at 0 degrees and which is at 180 degrees.

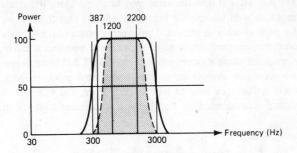

Figure 5-10
A High-Speed Asynchronous Modem, Bell Type 202

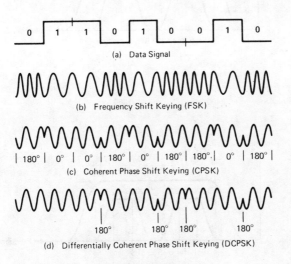

(a) Data Signal

(b) Frequency Shift Keying (FSK)

(c) Coherent Phase Shift Keying (CPSK)

(d) Differentially Coherent Phase Shift Keying (DCPSK)

Figure 5-11
Modulation Types

Another variant of this technique is shown in Figure 5-11d. Here the phase shift, rather than the absolute phase, is used to signify the signal element being transmitted. In the example shown a *1* is represented by a zero phase shift, a *0* by a 180 degree phase shift *from the previous signal element*. This latter technique, called differentially coherent phase-shift keying (DCPSK), is used in the Bell Type 212A asynchronous modem. This modem uses signalling frequencies of 1200 Hz and 2400 Hz and can be used in the full-duplex mode over a standard telephone line. Figure 5-12 shows the frequency arrangements. The Type 212A actually uses four possible phase angles for its signalling, rather than the two possibilities shown in Figure 5-11. The 212A can also be used asynchronously at 0 to 300 baud. Here it uses the same system as the Type 103 modem.

The problem with phase-shift keying systems is that there is no standard protocol for such systems at present. Until such a protocol is established (either by international agreement (or more likely by some one firm's making a large number of modems using its own protocol, as AT&T has done in the past) the chances are good that asynchronous phase-modulated modems from different manufacturers will not be able to talk to each other. For example, the 1200-baud signalling scheme used by Racal-Vadic is different from the Bell 212A system.

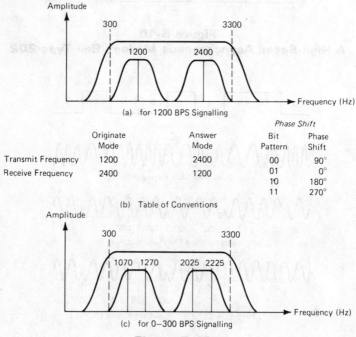

(a)   for 1200 BPS Signalling

	Originate Mode	Answer Mode	Phase Shift	
			Bit Pattern	Phase Shift
Transmit Frequency	1200	2400	00	90°
Receive Frequency	2400	1200	01	0°
			10	180°
			11	270°

(b)   Table of Conventions

(c)   for 0–300 BPS Signalling

Figure 5-12
Frequency Allocations for the Bell Type 212A Modem

The RS-232C Interface

Most of the modems in use today, and most other serial data exchange setups, follow an interface standard reached by agreement among the Bell System, the Electronic Industry Association, and various other interested manufacturers. This standard is known as RS-232C, where the "C" indicates the most recent revision. There are more recent standards, to which newer communications equipment will ultimately adhere, namely RS-422 and RS-423. The most overt manifestation of the RS-232C interface likely to be encountered by the microcomputer owner or designer is the 25-pin plug (or socket) to which the communications cable is attached. This standard connector is called a DB-25 connector. A drawing of the DB-25 connector layout is provided in Figure 5-13. Table 5-1 shows the pin assignments of the DB-25.

In most personal computers and similar microcomputers with simple serial interfaces, only three of the leads are connected: data send, data receive, and signal ground. This can cause a number of problems in situations where it is necessary to have some form of "handshaking" in the communication process. In such cases it is necessary to have a more sophisticated interface.

In particular, it is desirable to have the signals marked with asterisks available to the computer for telephone communications, or for direct intercomputer communications in which the status of the other computer at any given moment is uncertain.

As can be seen from Table 5-1, a primary purpose of the RS-232C standard is to define the types of signals to be used for data communications. The standard also specifies the electrical characteristics at the interface. For example, the mark (or *1*) signal is to be more negative than −3 volts with respect to signal ground, and the space (or *0*) signal is to be more positive than +3 volts with respect to signal ground. Anything between −3 volts and +3 volts is considered garbage. Details on the RS-232 and other EIA standards can be obtained from the Electronic Industries Association, 2001 Eye Street, N.W., Washington, D.C. 20006.

Figure 5-14 shows the equivalent circuit of an RS-232C signal line. The driver side of the line is seen as an AC generator with an output resistance shunted by an output capacitance (that is, a simple low-pass filter). The terminator side of the line is similar, except that the AC signal generator is replaced by a DC bias source (which is not to exceed 2 volts). The driver voltage is not to exceed 25 volts and the driver circuit should be able to sustain a short circuit without damaging itself or any other equipment. Most, if not all, commercially

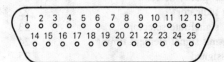

Figure 5-13
DB-25 Connector Layout

available U.S.-made modems meet the electrical and mechanical requirements of RS-232C. However, not all modems, and definitely not all microcomputers, are capable of handling the variety of signals covered in Table 5-1. For example, many microcomputers require that only pins 2, 3, and 7 be connected between the computer and its console. Some modems can handle current-loop signals; others cannot. Most low-cost modems have no provision for signal-element timing, because such signals are used only for synchronous communications. The point of all this is that before you purchase a modem, you should make sure that it will handle all the signals you want it to handle.

There is one important point to remember about connecting an external modem to a microcomputer via a pair of RS-232C connectors. The terms "trans-

Table 5-1
DB-25 Signal Lines for RS-232 Interface

Description	DB-25 Connector Number
Protective ground	1
Transmitted data*	2
Received data*	3
Request to send*	4
Clear to send*	5
Data set ready*	6
Signal ground*	7
Carrier detect*	8
(Reserved for testing)	9
(Reserved for testing)	10
Unassigned	11
Secondary carrier detect**	12
Secondary clear to send**	13
Secondary transmitted data**	14
Transmission sig. elem. timing	15
Secondary received data**	16
Receiver signal element timing	17
Unassigned	18
Secondary request to send**	19
Data terminal ready*	20
Signal quality detector	21
Ring indicator*	22
Data signal rate selector	23
Transmit signal element timing	24
Unassigned	25

*Used for modems
**Used for current-loop connections

mitted" and "received" in the description of RS-232C connector refer to the external terminal with which the computer is working. That is, pin 2 of the RS-232C connector handles data *transmitted by* the external data communication equipment, whatever it may be. Your computer must treat that signal as a *received* signal. Hence, unless the computer interface is already modified for use specifically with modems, the cable connecting your computer and the modem must have the wire from pin 2 of the computer going to pin 3 of the modem connector (or to pin 3 of the receiving computer if you are hard wiring them through RS-232C connectors), and vice versa. Figure 5-15a shows the arrangement. Cables wired in this manner are commonly called "null" cables.

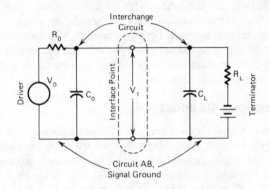

Figure 5-14
Equivalent Circuit for RS-232C

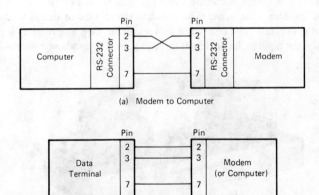

(a) Modem to Computer

(b)   Data Terminal to Modem (or Computer)

Figure 5-15
Minimum Cable Connections

The RS-449 and Other Serial Interface Standards

As mentioned earlier, the EIA has developed a more recent set of standards, designed to accommodate more effectively the growing variety of analog telecommunications methods. The governing standard is RS-449. In RS-449 data interchange signals and control signals are on separate circuits. Further, RS-449 uses two sets of connectors, one containing 37 pins, the other containing 9 pins. There are two companion standards, RS-422A and RS-423A. RS-422A deals with balanced-voltage digital interfaces as normally used with microelectronic circuits (the RS-232C system is an unbalanced-voltage system). RS-423A deals with unbalanced-voltage digital interfaces used with microelectronic circuits. All of these standards are compatible with RS-232C systems. One of the most important effects of the new standards is to increase the distance over which a computer and terminal or modem can communicate with each other. Since this is probably not a primary consideration for most microcomputer owners, and since the RS-232C standard is much more often encountered, these new standards will not be treated further here.

The Telephone Connection

Up to this point we have been talking about the preliminary aspects of converting a digital signal into one transmittable over the telephone lines and vice versa. There is one last stage to go through before the signal actually gets to the telephone line. In that last step it is necessary, by FCC rule, to ensure that the signal transmitted by the modem is electrically compatible with the telephone line. There are two ways to do this.

The easiest and least expensive method is to use the telephone handset as the interface with the telephone line. The handset works with an "acoustic-coupled" modem. That is, the modem output signal is fed to a small loudspeaker which is at the "talk" end of a cradle into which the telephone receiver is placed. Similarly, the input to the modem is through a small microphone which is located

Figure 5-16
Photograph of an Acoustic-Coupler Modem
(Courtesy of Micromate Electronics, Inc.)

at the receiver end of the telephone cradle. A typical acoustic-coupled modem is shown in Figure 5-16. In this arrangement the electrical signals to and from the modem are converted to acoustical signals to and from the handset. Since the handset is, presumably, already built to conform to FCC interconnect regulations, there is no further problem with that aspect of the data communication system.

There can be other problems, however. The signal-to-noise ratio of an acoustic-coupled modem is generally not as high as that of a direct-coupled modem. That means that, if you are communicating over a noisy telephone line, or one with a weak signal, the chances are higher that you will lose some data. In extreme cases you may not even be able to communicate at all. The communications interface, the telephone handset, responds to sound, so it also may respond to vibration of the modem cradle or to loud room noises, causing data errors. Manufacturers of acoustic modems go to some lengths to isolate the handset from external noises, usually by means of soft rubber pads connecting the handset to the modem.

The other means of connecting the modem to the telephone line is through a DAA. As was previously mentioned, this is simply a set of circuits which ensure that the output voltages from the modem do not exceed FCC limits and that only the allowed frequencies are transmitted on the telephone lines. In the late 1970s DAAs were usually separate devices which the microcomputer owner had to buy in addition to the modem circuits. Now, most of the modems sold for "built-in" use with microcomputers include an FCC-approved DAA. A typical example of a modem board, with DAA, for a microcomputer is shown in Figure 5-17.

Figure 5-17
Photograph of a Modem Board (D.C. Hayes)
(Courtesy of Hayes Microcomputer Products, Inc.)

The modem-cum-DAA is a separate device from the conventional telephone handset, and a federal regulation requires that the telephone company be informed when a modem is connected to the line. Simply call the telephone company and tell them that a modem is to be connected to the telephone line; also tell the ring frequency of the modem and the FCC approval number of the DAA, which should be printed on the modem.

The Parallel Connection: IEEE-488

Although we have been concerned primarily with communication over the telephone line with a serial asynchronous modem, there are many cases in which a parallel interface is more desirable, as was mentioned in Chapter 2. The IEEE-488 interface bus is commonly used in instrumentation systems, and in at least one series of microcomputers for parallel communications. Figure 5-18 shows the general concept of the IEEE-488 bus, also known as the General Purpose Information Bus (GPIB). As with other standards referenced here, there is an international standard version of the bus. It is governed by the International Electrotechnical Commission (IEC) Publication 625-1.

The bus consists of two sets of 8-bit parallel signal lines plus appropriate ground and shielding wires. One set of the signal lines is reserved for data transmission among the controlling computer and the devices attached to the bus. Data are transmitted a byte at a time rather than a bit at a time. This is known as "bit parallel, byte serial" communication. The other lines are used for determining the status of the attached devices and for controlling them.

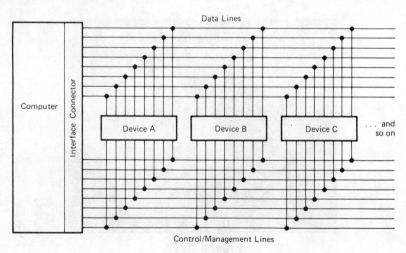

Figure 5-18
General Purpose Interface Bus (IEEE-488)

The inhabitants of the bus are grouped into two categories: talkers and listeners—just like a telephone conversation on a party line (more about that later). The computer (usually) controls the communications between itself and the devices by means of signals on the management lines. It can also be a listener or a talker, as can the attached devices. To get an idea of the process, consider the functions of the eight control/management lines. They are:

- **ATN** (Attention)—This line is used (only by the computer/controller) to signal the attached devices to pay attention to forthcoming information.

- **DAV** (Data Valid)—This line is used by any of the talkers to signal that it has put data on the data lines. Designated Listeners take heed.

- **EOI** (End or Identify)—This line is used by a talker to signal that the byte currently on the data lines is the last one to be sent.

- **IFC** (Interface Clear)—This line is used (only by the controller) to put the devices on the bus in a prearranged state of activity (or dormancy).

- **NDAC** (Not Data Accepted)—A listener busily gathering data from the data lines uses this line to indicate same.

- **NRFD** (Not Ready for Data)—A listener that is busy doing something else keeps a signal on this line until it is ready for more data.

- **REN** (Remote Enable)—This line lets a device other than the main controller do some controlling. Ordinarily the computer keeps this one off.

- **SRQ** (Support Required)—Any device needing some sort of support or action from the controller signals with this line.

As you can gather from this list, the process of using the GPIB hinges around the development of software to handle the various "handshaking" routines necessary to pass information along the bus. As you may also conclude, the IEEE-488 bus was developed primarily for communicating between computers and "smart" instruments in laboratories and manufacturing operations. The reader is referred to other books on the GPIB for further details.

6

If you happen to be content with connecting to a distant computer using a "dumb" terminal, a simple modem and a telephone line and if you are happy to have the distant computer do all the computations and store all the information you will need—then you will be quite happy with a very simple telecommunications system, and need read no further. If, on the other hand, you are interested in using a microcomputer to do more sophisticated telecommunications tasks, such as transferring files between machines, engaging in computer conferencing, or handling electronic mail—and to do some of these automatically—then you will quickly discover the great software trap.

THE NEED FOR SOFTWARE

All the sophisticated hardware of your computer, as you know, is useless without sophisticated software to make it run in accordance with your wishes. The same is definitely true when you try to get your microcomputer to talk to others. Without the proper software controlling them, the telecommunications components added to the microcomputer system are useless. The purpose of this chapter and the next two is to demonstrate, in graduated steps, how you can develop or adapt telecommunications software to suit your communications needs, starting with the fundamental features that every telecommunications program must have, then expanding to more diverse and specialized features and to specific alterations you must make to communicate with a variety of different systems.

Unfortunately, one of the most prevalent characteristics of the contemporary market in microcomputers is the diversity of methods for controlling I/O (input and output) functions. Consequently, no book such as this can hope to cover the details of the techniques required to run all possible microcomputer-modem combinations. This book, instead, will first cover each of the steps in the development of some representative software packages, in terms of a functional analysis of the purpose of the software module, then present one or more representative ways of performing that function in BASIC or Z80 assembly language. BASIC will be used because it is the high level language most commonly used in personal computers, although it is not necessarily the best for telecommunications software ("C" or FORTH might be less subject to timing worries at data rates above 300 baud, for example). Z80 assembler is used for two reasons: First, because the 8080-Z80 family of microprocessors is used in the greatest variety of 1982-vintage personal computers; second, because these microprocessors are the ones with which the author is most familiar. In any case,

Hardware Isn't Enough

---

the step-by-step treatment should allow you to make suitable modifications to suit your own circumstances, regardless of the particular hardware-software combination you are using.

ASCII: THE LINGUA FRANCA OF "COMPUTICATIONS"

Before we go rushing pell-mell into the jungle of software design, let's briefly investigate the basic code used by most computers with which you are likely to communicate. It is known as ASCII, for "American Standard for Computer Information Interchange." It is pronounced *asky*. This particular code (or minor variations of it) is also known as the ISO code, International Standard 646, and CCITT Alphabet Number 5.*

ASCII code ordinarily uses binary words seven bits in length. It is therefore capable of transmitting 128 different characters. Unfortunately, not all letters and common punctuation marks of the alphabets of all nations fit into 128 spaces. Therefore, the symbols represented by some of the ASCII words (where a "word" is seven bits) may mean one thing in the United States and something quite different in other countries. There are other computer information interchange codes beside ASCII. The most common of these is an eight-bit code known as EBCDIC (often pronounced *ebb-see-dik*), for "Extended Binary-Coded-Decimal Interchange Code." This code, with 256 possible characters, is used primarily by IBM equipment.

ASCII code is usually represented in a table containing eight columns and sixteen rows, given here (Table 6-1) with the rows and column headings in both binary and hexadecimal form. Note that the binary headings of the columns all start with "X" to point out that, for ASCII seven-bit codes, it does not really matter whether the most significant bit in an eight-bit word is a *0* or a *1*. I will adopt the convention here that the *most significant bit* in a byte (the leftmost one as it appears in printed form) is called *bit 7*. The least significant bit (the rightmost one) is called *bit 0*. The ASCII word always occupies the least-significant-bit positions, that is, bits 6 through 0 (generally, the most significant bit is assumed to be 0). In order to piece together an eight-bit word in ASCII code from the table, use the binary column heading followed by the binary row

---

* CCITT is the International Consultative Committee for Telephone and Telegraph, the international body that recommends communications standards, as mentioned in Chapter 5.

heading. Thus the character 'L' in the fourth column and twelfth row would read *01001100* (or *11001100*) in binary, *4C* (or *CC*) in hex.

Aside from the recognizable numbers, letters, and punctuation marks in columns 2 through 7, there are multi-letter symbols in the first two columns. These symbols generally represent machine activities rather than printable characters. They are used to control the computer, so they are often known to users as "Control-" signals; they are generated on the keyboard by simultaneously depressing a "Control" or "CTRL" key and a key from column 4 (for column 0) or 5 (for 1) of Table 6-1. The function of the CTRL key is to make bit 6 a *0*. Thus, when "CTRL-Y" is keyed, the microcomputer sends X0*011001* (or EM in Table 6-1) instead of X1*011001* (again, the 'X' could be a *0* or a *1* depending on the microcomputer). Table 6-2 gives more complete definitions of the usual control uses of the symbols in the first two columns.

These two tables give the ASCII symbols for U.S. usage. There are differences in some of the symbols in other countries. For example:

- The "#" sign is used in most countries to represent kilograms. It is not used as an abbreviation for the word "number." The British replace this symbol with a "£" (pound) sign.

- The "$" sign is used only in the U.S., Canada, and a few other countries. In many countries this is replaced by their own or a universal symbol for currency.

Table 6-1
ASCII Code

Binary	Hex	X000 0(8)	X001 1(9)	X010 2(A)	X011 3(B)	X100 4(C)	X101 5(D)	X110 6(E)	X111 7(F)
0000	0	NUL	DLE	SP	0	@	P	'	p
0001	1	SOH	DC1	!	1	A	Q	a	q
0010	2	STX	DC2	"	2	B	R	b	r
0011	3	ETX	DC3	#	3	C	S	c	s
0100	4	EOT	DC4	$	4	D	T	d	t
0101	5	ENQ	NAK	%	5	E	U	e	u
0110	6	ACK	SYN	&	6	F	V	f	v
0111	7	BEL	ETB	'	7	G	W	g	w
1000	8	BS	CAN	(	8	H	X	h	x
1001	9	HT	EM	)	9	I	Y	i	y
1010	A	LF	SUB	*	:	J	Z	j	z
1011	B	VT	ESC	+	;	K	[	k	{
1100	C	FF	FS	,	<	L	\	l	|
1101	D	CR	GS	–	=	M	]	m	}
1110	E	SO	RS	.	>	N	∧	n	~
1111	F	SI	US	/	?	O	—	o	DEL

- The symbols in rows B through E in the fifth and seventh columns of Table 6-1 are used for national differences in symbols. For example, in Belgium, France, Switzerland, and Italy, the U.S. symbol "}" becomes "é".

These distinctions may not be important if you are planning to communicate only within the U.S. If you are, or may be, communicating with other countries it is likely that your computer should have appropriate provisions in its software to allow for these differences when printing the information received or sending the proper text forms.

As for the CTRL/communications symbols, there is great variation in how these are used by different computer manufacturers and software houses. Some of these symbols are common to almost all computers and software packages, particularly those used for device control. These are BEL, BS, HT, LF, VT, FF and CR. Unfortunately, the fact that these *symbols* are found in most systems does not mean that they necessarily result in the same *actions* on each system. For example, the LF on one system may simply move the cursor (on a CRT display) or the carriage (on a printer) down one line without changing its horizontal position. On another system the LF may also cause a return to the first position on the next line, equivalent to a LF-then-CR combination.

Table 6-2
Control Symbols

Symbol	Hex Value	Char. Used with CTRL	Meaning	Symbol	Hex Value	Char. Used with CTRL	Meaning
NUL	00	@	null (blank)	DLE	10	P	data link escape
SOH	01	A	start of header	DC1	11	Q	device control 1
STX	02	B	start of text	DC2	12	R	device control 2
ETX	03	C	end of text	DC3	13	S	device control 3
EOT	04	D	end transmission	DC4	14	T	dev. ct. 4—stop
ENQ	05	E	enquiry	NAK	15	U	negative acknowl.
ACK	06	F	Acknowledge (pos.)	SYN	16	V	synchronization
BEL	07	G	bell	ETB	17	W	end text block
BS	08	H	backspace	CAN	18	X	cancel
HT	09	I	horiz. tab	EM	19	Y	end of medium
LF	0A	J	line feed	SUB	1A	Z	substitute
VT	0B	K	vertical tab	ESC	1B	[	escape
FF	0C	L	form feed	FS	1C	\	file separator
CR	0D	M	carriage return	GS	1D	]	group separator
SO	0E	N	shift out	RS	1E	∧	record separator
SI	0F	O	shift in	US	1F	—	unit separator

The rest of the symbols appear on some computers and not on others (ESC, for example), generally at the whim of the manufacturer. The effects of others, such as the device control symbols (DC1 through DC4), are particularly dependent on the details of the computer system. As we shall see later, these variations constitute one of the major impediments to the design of a "universal" software package for computer telecommunications.

Although these caveats may sound ominous, it is clear that a great deal of computer communications succeeds in spite of some of the irritations of this lack of a true set of standard forms. In general, the problem for a would-be computer communicator is to be aware that these variations exist, particularly in the control codes, find out which set is used in the computer to be communicated with (presumably she already knows which is used in her own), and make sure that the software used for communications supports the particular idiosyncracies of the two (or more) systems. The following sections will describe, among other things, how to go about this task.

MINIMUM REQUIREMENTS: THE MICROCOMPUTER AS A DUMB TERMINAL

The first communication task to explore is the use of the microcomputer as a "dumb" terminal. This term is used because in this mode the microcomputer behaves exactly like a simple CRT terminal or teletypewriter; it simply sends the information typed into its keyboard and displays information received from outside—it does nothing else. If the microcomputer were to operate solely in this mode it could easily be replaced by a true dumb terminal. However, we will later see how to enhance the capabilities of the communication software, starting from this dumb core of hardware and operating software, so that the system can perform much more complicated tasks. The following sections assume that your microcomputer and related telecommunications equipment are of the sort readily available commercially in the United States. "Home brew" systems, or systems from other countries, may not perform in the same way.

Required Hardware

Unless your microcomputer has a built-in telecommunications capability, a few items are needed to form a communicating microcomputer. These are:

Type 1: External Modem

1. The microcomputer itself, with a display of some sort.

2. A serial (RS-232) interface board internal to the microcomputer for communicating with the outside world.

3. A "null" cable for connecting the serial interface to the modem. Remember, a null cable interchanges pins 2 and 3 of the RS-232 connector to make the microcomputer appear to the modem as a dumb terminal. If the microcom-

puter-modem connection works with a standard, uninterchanged interconnecting cable, don't change it.

4. A separate modem. This may be an acoustic-coupled or direct-connect device. For the time being, the explanation will assume an acoustic-coupled modem. Therefore, you also need a telephone to use with it.

Type 2: Internal Modem

1. The microcomputer, as above, of a variety that will accept additional plug-in circuit boards.

2. A modem board, of a variety that will work in your microcomputer.

3. A DAA (see Chapter 5) for isolating the microcomputer and the telephone line from each other. Often this is included in commercially available modem-board packages. Remember: you cannot legally operate a direct-connect modem in the U.S. without one of these.

4. A connector cable with a modular or other plug suitable for connecting to your telephone line.

With this set of equipment you have the basic capability to communicate with almost any computer in the world, if the intervening telephone system is up to it.

Functions to be Performed

With an actual dumb terminal and acoustic modem, starting to communicate with an external computer is quite simple: you turn on the terminal, dial the number of the computer installation, listen for the tone from the answering computer, put the telephone receiver into the modem cradle, wait for the "carrier detect" signal to light up on the modem, then start communicating. The presence of the microcomputer makes that first step a little more complicated. The computer has to be set to engage in the prospective interchange by means of a communications software package. This package has to perform at least the following things:

• Set up the UART in the serial interface to run with the proper baud rate (the rate at which the modem is set to operate), the proper number of stop bits, and the proper parity.

• Select the proper duplex mode—that is, make the decision whether to display all characters keyed by the operator directly (half-duplex), or wait for the other computer to echo them (full-duplex).

• Set the computer so that everything that is typed on the keyboard, except one or two control codes, goes to the serial interface and so that everything from the serial interface, except possibly some control codes, gets displayed or printed.

- Establish the control codes for entering and leaving the communications program such that neither do they interfere with, nor are they accidentally received during, communications with the other computer.

- (Optional) Tell the operator that the computer is ready for communication.

If all these functions are in the communications software package, then it can be expected to communicate with most computers that are already set up for operation with remote terminals. The only additional step, beyond those required with a dumb terminal, is that the computer operator must run the communications program in addition to turning on the computer and the modem.

In some systems some communications parameters, particularly the baud rate, the type of parity, and the type of duplex, are set by switches on the hardware rather than by software commands.

SAMPLE COMMUNICATIONS PROGRAMS

These straightforward functional requirements can be translated into program requirements just as easily. As Figure 6-1 shows, there are only two main parts to the core telecommunications program, or to a much more sophisticated one, for that matter. These are the initialization module and the communications module. The initialization module has the task of making sure that the system— the computer, the interface and, indirectly, the modem—are all coordinated and ready to communicate. The communications module has the task of handling the actual communications and, as we shall see later, any other related tasks the operator might desire, including stopping the communication sequence.

INITIALIZATION MODULE. The initialization module is quite straightforward, as seen in Figure 6-2. In the simple system under consideration

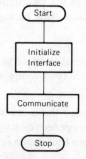

Figure 6-1
Core Program Flow Chart

now the initializer has really only two things to do: make sure that the proper command is put together to set up the interface to the modem, and make sure that the interface is not doing something else. It can also inform the computer operator that it is ready by means of some sort of message to be displayed when all its other tasks have been completed.

The details of the content of these messages depend on the particular computer and interface hardware being used. In particular, the interface board is "located," in terms of the logical arrangement of the computer, at some I/O port. That is, the computer sends characters to, and receives characters from, the interface at a certain port address (the functional equivalent of a mailbox). In some computers the address is fixed; there is no way the user can change it. In others the address may be changeable either by software or, more likely, by a

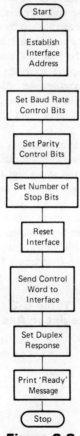

Figure 6-2
Initialization Module

set of switches on the interface board itself. Setting the switches causes the board to respond only to signals sent to its address. Similarly, each time the board receives a signal from the modem it notifies the computer of the fact by setting a "flag" at its interface port (the "data available" flag in Figure 5-5), analogously to the postman's raising the flag on a rural mailbox when mail has been delivered. In any case, the software must know the address of the interface board so that all subsequent communications are addressed to it rather than to some other unit in the computer.

The other detail with which the intialization routine must concern itself is the arrangement of status and/or control bits in the "word" that goes to the interface board to control it. The previously mentioned switches for the interface board set the "base" address of the board. This is the address of the first register of the interface, typically either the status or the data register. Interface boards and internal modems can have several registers, each of which is addressable as an *offset* from the base address established by the switches on the board. The status and the control register of a simple interface board are often at the same address (the same offset from the base address). The control register works through the *output* port; the computer sends the data determining the communication parameters *to* it. The status register works through the *input* port; the computer gets data *from* it to determine the status of the communications process. The data register is used for both input (data received) and output (data to be sent).

Although each bit in the status register may mean something important, the specific significance of each bit varies from manufacturer to manufacturer. As an example, Table 6-3 displays the status-register bit assignment for the Cromemco TUART™, the Radio Shack TRS-80™ interface board, and for the D.C. Hayes (80-103A™ and the Micromodem 100™) internal modems. It is clear from the table that each hardware system must have its own special bit patterns for checking status. Table 6-3 can be translated to a bit pattern as follows. A 1 in the bit position shown in the table for a given board indicates that the function shown holds. For example, if the Cromemco TUART status register were to

Table 6-3
Typical Register Assignments

Function	Bit Assignment Cromemco	TRS-80	Hayes
Transmitter Buffer Empty	7	6	1
Read Data Available	6	7	0
Parity Error	—	3	2
Framing Error	0	4	3
Overrun Error	1	5	4
Start Bit Detect	4	—	—

return a 11000000 (C0 hexadecimal) it would indicate that it had received a character from the modem, had no characters to transmit and detected no errors. A D. C. Hayes modem would give a reverse pattern, 00000011, while the TRS-80 would also respond with 11000000, but only because the two elements are interchanged in the same two locations as the Cromemco system. A similar lack of standardization holds true for the interface control registers.

COMMUNICATION MODULE. The initialization module seems straightforward in concept but tricky in detail. The communication module seems much more complicated in concept but is relatively simple to implement since the tricky details are taken care of in the initializer. Figure 6-3 shows the general schema of a simple communications module. It consists of a single main routine and a pair of subsidiary routines.

The main routine has two functions: to decide whether there is a character to be sent or to be received, and to keep listening otherwise. In structured form this would read:

REPEAT the following sequence;
    WHILE the console has a character AND there has been no ABORT signal from the console
        GET the character from the console character cruncher;
    END of the console loop;
    WHILE the modem interface has a character
        GET the character from the modem character cruncher;
    END of the modem loop;
UNTIL there is an ABORT signal from the console.

The purpose of the "character cruncher" routines is to fetch the characters from either the keyboard or the modem, see if there are any special characters that must be dealt with (either by ignoring them or making something out of the ordinary happen), and display the rest. One important function of these routines is to prevent undesirable things from happening, such as a control character's being sent to the external computer via the modem that would cause the external computer to drop the connection. The other important function of the keyboard-character processor (console character cruncher) is to check for the control characters that allow the communications process to be revised (as we shall see in the next chapter) or intentionally terminated (aborted).

Analyzing a Sample Communications Program

There is a program on page 89, written in Cromemco 32K Structured BASIC, that performs the functions just described, except for one. It does not check for control characters other than the one that will terminate the program. Since the particular dialect of BASIC that is used here includes the constructs of structured programming, the program follows that format.

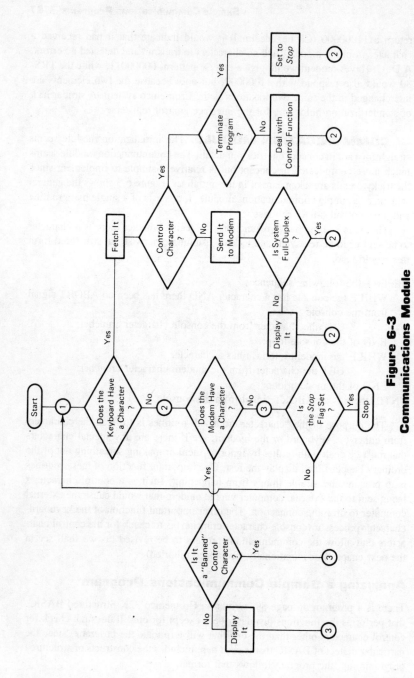

**Figure 6-3
Communications Module**

```
5     Imode : X=0.1234 : If X>0 Then Run
10    Rem The above sets the computer to integer arithmetic mode
15    Rem  -- and resets it if it doesn't work the first time
20    Rem  The purpose is to save memory space and slightly increase
25    Rem  the speed of execution.
30    Set 0,-1 : Rem This inhibits automatic CR-LFs from BASIC
35    Rem
40    Rem ***************** BASIC Modem Driver *********************
45    Rem
50    Rem This is written in Cromemco 32K Structured BASIC
55    Rem  - other BASICs may have slightly different formats
60    Rem * This program is for use with an acoustic coupler modem
65    Rem   set at port address 00C0H (192 decimal)
70    Rem   but may be used with other modems with only minor changes.

75    Rem ------------------------------------------------------------
80    Rem               First Part: Initialization
85    Rem ------------------------------------------------------------
90    Rem                        ** SET UP **
95    Rem -- First, establish the addresses of the I/O ports:
100   Statport=%00C0% : Rem The "%" signs enclose hexadecimal numbers
105   Rem The base I/O port address, to which the I/O board is switched,
110   Rem is C0 (hexadecimal). Any other port may be used that is not
115   Rem in conflict with other functions of your computer.
120   Constat=0 : Rem Console status port
125   Consdata=1 : Rem Console data port
130   Baudport=Statport : Rem This port is used to set the baud rate
135   Dataport=Statport+1 : Rem This is the I/O data port
140   Comndport=Statport+2 : Rem This is used to send commands to the I/O
145   Rem                  board - the control register
150   Intrtport=Statport+3 : Rem This is the I/O interrupt register
155   Rem                   ----------------
160   Sayonara=4 : Rem 4 = Control-D; used to terminate the program
165   Lfeed=10 : Rem ASCII value for line feed character
170   Rem --  Next set the baud rate byte
175   Baudbyte=%0084% : Rem With the Cromemco TUART this sets the baud
180   Rem            rate to 300, with one stop bit and 8 data bits,
185   Rem            when this byte is sent to Baudport.
190   Reset=1 : Rem This byte, when sent to Comndport, resets the TUART
195   Inhibint=0 : Rem This byte will inhibit interrupts when sent to the
200   Rem            interrupt register

205   Rem                        ** DO IT! **
210   Out Baudport,Baudbyte : Rem This command format : Out A,B sends
215   Rem                  byte B to port A.
220   Out Comndport,Reset
225   Out Intrtport,Inhibint
230   Dupflag=-1 : Rem This sets the program for full-duplex operation
235   Dataready=%0040% : Rem A 1 in bit 6 of the input status register
240   Rem            means that data has been received.
245   Transready=%0080% : Rem Similarly, a 1 in bit 7 means OK to send data
250   Quitflag=0 : Rem This is the flag that exits the program when it is set

255   Rem ------------------------------------------------------------
260   Rem               ****** MAIN PROGRAM ******
265   Rem ------------------------------------------------------------

270   Print"Intercomputer Telecommunications Program"
275   Print"Go ahead, please ---- Control-D will  stop  the program";Chr$(7)
280   Noesc : Rem This instruction prevents BASIC from constantly checking
285   Rem         the console for a character. We want the program to do it.
290     Repeat
295     Rem First check the console status and also for an ABORT signal from
296     Rem  the console
300       While Binand(Inp(Constat),Dataready) And Not Quitflag
305       Rem     Binand(A,B) performs a logical AND operation on the two
310       Rem     bytes A and B. In this case, byte A is the status byte
315       Rem     from the console I/O port.
320       Rem     Inp(X) acts to input a byte from port X.
325       Gosub Consproc : Rem If the console has a byte this routine
326       Rem processes it
330       Endwhile : Rem End of the console loop
335       While Binand(Inp(Statport),Dataready) : Rem check the modem status
340       Gosub Modemproc : Rem If there is a byte, process it
345       Endwhile : Rem End of the modem loop
350     Until Quitflag
```

```
355    Esc : Rem This turns the automatic console checking back on
360    Stop

365    Rem -----------------------------------------------------------------
370    Rem
375    Rem                 ######  SUBROUTINES  ######
380    Rem
385    Rem -----------------------------------------------------------------

390    #Consproc : Rem This routine processes ASCII characters from the console
395      Character=Inp(1) : Rem Get the character from the console data port
400      Character=Binand(Character,%007F%) : Rem Set the parity bit to 0
405      If Character=Sayonara Then Quitflag=-1 : Return : Rem Stop char. rec'd
410      If Character=Lfeed Then Return : Rem Don't send a line feed to the modem
415      Rem Wait until the modem is ready for the character

420    #Modcheck : If Binand(Inp(Statport),Transready)=0 Then Goto Modcheck
425      Out Dataport,Character : Rem Send the character to the modem
430      If Dupflag Then Return : Rem Don't echo the character if full-duplex
435      Print Chr$(Character); : Rem Otherwise echo it to the console
440      If Character=13 Then Print : Rem Add a line feed if it was a CR
445      Return

450    Rem -----------------------------------------------------------

455    #Modemproc : Rem This routine processes ASCII characters from the modem
460      Character=Inp(Dataport) : Rem Get the character from the modem
465      Character=Binand(Character,%007F%) : Rem Strip the parity bit
470      Badflag=0 : Gosub Badchar : Rem Check for banned characters
475      If Badflag Then Return : Rem Ignore the bad guys
480      Print Chr$(Character); : Rem Otherwise display it
485      Return
490      Rem                        ####

495    #Badchar : Rem This routine checks for undesirable characters
500      Rem This should be customized to your particular system
505      Rem The following rejects only Control- characters other than
510      Rem BEL,BS,HT,LF,VT,FF, CR, and ESCape
515      If Character>31 And Character<127 Then Return : Rem Print all letters,
516      Rem numbers, etc.
520      If Character<7 Then Badflag=-1 : Return
525      If Character>13 And Character<27 Then #Badflag=-1 : Return
530      If Character>27 Then Badflag=-1
535      Return

540 End
```

As you have already noticed, this dialect of BASIC has some features that may not be present in other dialects. For example, relatively long names can be assigned to variables so that they can be more easily read by humans. (The computer just uses one-byte "tokens" for these variables, ignoring all the rest of the characters.) Subroutines are called by name, not by a line number, also for easy reference. But these features, while making it easier for the programmer, do not alter the basic logic of the program, a logic that can be duplicated in most other dialects of BASIC. This program can be run as is on a Cromemco computer, or any computer using Cromemco 32K BASIC, with a Cromemco TUART or similar serial data interface board. The annotations for almost every instruction should allow the programmer to adapt it to other systems.

One problem with this program is that, although it will serve perfectly well for simple communications with another computer, it and the BASIC interpreter take up a considerable amount of the computer's memory. The program as written above—with all the remarks included—uses up 6656 bytes (to the nearest higher 128-byte boundary). The BASIC interpreter, as its title suggests, takes up 32K bytes. This is still no problem at this stage of evolution of the program because no additional memory is required to operate the program. It may become vexatious as we add features in the next chapter. The first step in reducing the size of the program is to delete all of the Rem(ark) statements since they add nothing to the actual operation of the program. This reduces its size to 1920 bytes! Quite an illustration of the cost of *overhead* that is used to improve program readability. Here is the unadorned program:

```
  5   Imode : X=0.1234 : If X>0 Then Run
 30   Set O,-1
100   Statport=%00C0%
120   Constat=0
125   Consdata=1
130   Baudport=Statport
135   Dataport=Statport+1
140   Comndport=Statport+2
150   Intrtport=Statport+3
160   Sayonara=4
165   Lfeed=10
175   Baudbyte=%0084%
190   Reset=1
195   Inhibint=0
210   Out Baudport,Baudbyte
220   Out Comndport,Reset
225   Out Intrtport,Inhibint
230   Dupflag=-1
235   Dataready=%0040%
245   Transready=%0080%
250   Quitflag=0

270   Print"Intercomputer Telecommunications Program"
275   Print"Go ahead, please ---- Control-D will  stop  the program";Chr$(7)
280   Noesc
290     Repeat
300       While Binand(Inp(Constat),Dataready) And Not Quitflag
325       Gosub Consproc
330       Endwhile
335       While Binand(Inp(Statport),Dataready)
340       Gosub Modemproc
345       Endwhile
350     Until Quitflag
355   Esc
360   Stop

390 #Consproc
395   Character=Inp(1)
400   Character=Binand(Character,%007F%)
405   If Character=Sayonara Then Quitflag=-1 : Return
410   If Character=Lfeed Then Return

420 #Modcheck : If Binand(Inp(Statport),Transready)=0 Then Goto Modcheck
425   Out Dataport,Character
430   If Dupflag Then Return
435   Print Chr$(Character);
440   If Character=13 Then Print
445   Return
455 #Modemproc
460   Character=Inp(Dataport)
465   Character=Binand(Character,%007F%)
470   Badflag=0 : Gosub Badchar
475   If Badflag Then Return
480   Print Chr$(Character);
485   Return

495 #Badchar
515   If Character>31 And Character<127 Then Return
520   If Character<7 Then Badflag=-1 : Return
525   If Character>13 And Character<27 Then Badflag=-1 : Return
530   If Character>27 Then Badflag=-1
535   Return

540 End
```

Another way to materially reduce the amount of space the software occupies during execution is to write the program in a language that compiles rather than interprets the code. This eliminates many popular versions of BASIC, because most of the so-called BASIC compilers actually compile to an intermediate code that still must be interpreted, even though this intermediate version is faster to interpret than the original BASIC code. Of course, the fastest and shortest version of a program is usually the one written in assembler. The following is a version of the communications program written in Z80 assembler code, complete with remarks as in the first BASIC program listed above.

```
            TITLE    MODEM-DISK I/O CONTROL FOR CROMEMCO CDOS & EXTERNAL COMPUTER
        ;
        ;        A basic modem program for
        ;        Cromemco CDOS, Version 1.07
        ;        and higher and acoustic coupler
        ;        modem operating from
        ;        TUART port 00COH
        ;        NOTE: Some of the instructions in this program
        ;              are system-dependent.  That is, the details
        ;              may change with other systems or hardware
        ;              configurations.  These are marked with
        ;              asterisks (*) in the comments column.
        ;
        ;
TRUE        EQU      -1
FALSE       EQU      0
DUPLEX      EQU      TRUE          ;TRUE for HALF-duplex
LFEED       EQU      FALSE         ;TRUE to transmit linefeeds
CDOS        EQU      5             ;Location of CDOS (and CP/M) system calls
        ;
        ;PORT ASSIGNMENTS
        ;
MSTATP      EQU      0COH          ;I/O status port (input)*
MBAUD       EQU      MSTATP        ;I/O baud rate port*
                                   ;  (output)
MDATA       EQU      MSTATP+1      ;I/O data port (I/O)*
MCMD        EQU      MSTATP+2      ;I/O command (control) register
                                   ;  (output)*
MINTR       EQU      MSTATP+3      ;I/O interrupt register
                                   ;  (I/O)*
        ;
        ;MISCELLANEOUS
CR          EQU      0DH           ;ASCII carriage return
LF          EQU      0AH           ;ASCII line feed
EOM         EQU      0FFH          ;End of message mask
CTRLD       EQU      04H           ;Control-D
ESC         EQU      1BH           ;ESCape
        ;
        ;
INIT:       LD       A,84H         ;Sets modem to 300 baud,*
            OUT      (MBAUD),A     ; one stop bit, 8 data bits
            LD       A,1           ;Reset I/O*
            OUT      (MCMD),A
            LD       A,0           ;Inhibit interrupts*
            OUT      (MINTR),A
            LD       (DUPFLG),A    ;Set to full duplex
            LD       HL,SIGN       ;Point to signon message
            CALL     PRINTM
        ;
        ;
        ;
        ;THIS IS THE MAIN PROGRAM LOOP
        ;
LOOP:       CALL     INSTAT        ;Get console status
            JR       NZ,CONIN      ;If byte available, get it
            IN       A,(MSTATP)    ;Get modem status
            BIT      6,A           ;Check for byte in receiver*
```

```
        JR      NZ,MODIN        ;If byte available, get it
        JR      LOOP            ;Else recycle
;
CONIN:  IN      A,(MSTATP)      ;Make sure modem's clear
        BIT     7,A             ;(i.e., ready to transmit)*
        JR      Z,CONIN         ;Wait until ready, then ...
        CALL    INPUT           ;Read console
        LD      C,A             ;Save the console character
        CP      CTRLD           ;Control-D?
        JR      Z,EXIT          ;If yes, quit!
        CALL    TRANS           ;Send, and echo the char.
                                ; if half-duplex
        JR      LOOP            ;Back to main loop
;
MODIN:  IN      A,(MDATA)       ;Get byte from modem
        AND     7FH             ;Kill parity bit
        LD      C,A             ;Save character
        CP      20H             ;Is it a "normal" character?
        JR      NC,MODIN1       ; If so, display it
        CP      7               ;Ignore control chars. <BEL*
        JR      C,LOOP
        CP      0EH             ;Pass others up to CR*
        JR      C,MODIN1
        CP      ESC             ;Also pass ESCape*
        JR      NZ,LOOP         ;But flush all other CCs*
MODIN1: CALL    OUTPUT          ;Display the survivors
        JR      LOOP
;
;
;PRINT MESSAGE UNTIL EOM CHARACTER
;
PRINTM: LD      A,EOM
        LD      C,(HL)          ;Get a byte from the buffer
        CP      C               ;Test for EOM (End Of
                                ;Message)
        RET     Z               ;If so, we're finished
        CALL    OUTPUT          ;Else, print it
        INC     HL              ;Point to the next byte
        JR      PRINTM          ;Loop again
;
;THIS SUBROUTINE SENDS A BYTE TO THE MODEM
;
TRANS:  IN      A,(MSTATP)      ;Check the modem again
        BIT     7,A             ;*
        JR      Z,TRANS         ;Loop until ready
TRANS1: IN      A,(MSTATP)      ;Check to see if ext. compt'r is ready
        BIT     6,A             ; First, check for char. from ext. compt'r*
        JR      Z,TRANS2        ; If none, press on
        IN      A,(MDATA)       ; If so, get the character
        AND     7FH             ; Strip parity bit
        CP      11H             ; Go ahead signal (^-Q)?*
        JR      Z,TRANS2        ; Do so
        CP      13H             ; Is it a busy signal? NOTE: This may vary
                                ;   among different computer systems*
        JR      Z,TRANS1        ; If so, wait until clear
TRANS2: LD      A,C             ;Get the local byte
    IF NOT LFEED
        CP      LF              ;Don't send linefeed to modem
        JR      Z,TRANS3
    ENDIF
        OR      80H             ;Add MARK parity to byte*
                                ;NOTE: The above may be omitted if the
                                ; other computer is indifferent to
                                ; parity
        OUT     (MDATA),A       ;Send the byte
        LD      A,(DUPFLG)      ;Check for half duplex
        CP      0FFH
        LD      A,C             ;If not, ignore console
        RET     NZ
TRANS3: AND     7FH             ;Take the parity bit off
        CALL    OUTPUT          ; and send to the console
        RET
;
EXIT:   DI                      ;First, disable interrupts
        IM      2               ;Set to Z80 interrupt mode 2
```

```
        LD      HL,7CH      ; so that the operating
        LD      SP,HL       ; system can be immediately
        LD      A,O         ; reentered
        LD      I,A         ;Then ...
        JP      O           ;Do it!
;
;I/O ROUTINES---------------------$
;
OUTPUT: LD      E,C         ;Get character
        LD      C,2         ;Set up CDOS
        CALL    CDOS        ;Send char. to console
        RET
;
INSTAT: IN      A,O         ;Get console status
        AND     40H         ;Check data available bit$
        RET     Z           ;Character not ready
        LD      A,-1
        RET                 ; -1 if character ready
;
INPUT:  IN      A,1         ;Get character from the
        AND     7FH         ; console
        RET
;
DUPFLG: DEFS    1           ;Half/full-duplex flag
;
SIGN:   DB      CR,LF,LF
        DB      'Modem control program'
        DB      CR,LF,O,O
        DB      '(Control-D returns you to CDOS)',CR,LF,EOM
;
        END     INIT
```

This program, when assembled, occupies a mere 247 bytes! Furthermore, it doesn't need anything else, such as an external interpreter, to run properly. However, assembly language programs are much more tedious and time-consuming to write and, especially, maintain than are programs using interpreters. The extra time taken in revising and debugging each version after even trivial changes can run into hours—or even days and weeks for complicated programs. One such trivial change, in the version above, is going from full- to half-duplex operation. Here the program must be reassembled, after an entry is added in the initialization so that it will read:

$$LD \quad A, -1$$

$$LD \quad (DUPFLG),A$$

This is a good reason to write the first attempts at a new program in an interpreter language, such as BASIC, keeping as close to a structured format as possible. Then, when you are assured that everything works properly, rewrite it in assembler if you feel that you need the space or that the BASIC program is too slow.

As can be seen from the example, however, the assembly-language program has to be concerned with all the tedious details that are hidden in a higher-level language. Even in the example, though, some of the tedious details are still hidden. The reason we can avoid a few of the nit-picking problems is that some of the I/O (input/output) instructions are taken care of by the operating system of the computer.

INTERACTION WITH AN OPERATING SYSTEM

The operating system of the microcomputer used for communication—and of the computer with which it is communicating—can help in taking care of many of the bothersome details of the communications process. Unfortunately, the operating systems can also cause significant impediments to the communication process.

In the first program given here, the BASIC interpreter takes care of the details of operating-system interaction. None of it is visible to the programmer, at least at this stage of program development. In the assembly-language program just shown, however, there are some direct interfaces with the operating system in the I/O routines. The three I/O routines shown deal with "system calls." These are specific commands to the computer operating system to handle input/output functions—in this case, those dealing with the system console.

System Calls

A system call is a technique whereby a program can have the operating system perform some standard housekeeping function, typically by placing a specific number in one of the microprocessor's registers and then causing the system to go into action by CALLing a standard address. The operating system, when called by this technique, checks the register and then performs the function associated with the number left in the register. In CP/M® and similar operating systems the C register is used for the system call. The address used for the CALL command in these operating systems is 5. Frequently another register is used as well in order to pass a parameter or character to the operating system. For example, in the OUTPUT routine above, the character to be displayed on the console is put in the E register and the call number, 2, is put in the C register. The operating system, upon receiving system call 2, displays whatever is in the E register on the console. As we shall see in the next chapter, similar simple techniques can be used to access more complicated operations, such as creation and retrieval of files on a disk.

The reason it is desirable to use system calls is that they make it more likely (but not absolutely certain) that a program written for one type of computer can also be used on another type, provided they use the same operating system. The use of system calls acts to isolate the details of system operation from the applications program. Thus, system A, with two 5-1/4" single-sided single-density floppy disk drives and terminal brand X, can easily use a program written for system B, which has 8" double-sided double-density floppies, a hard disk, and CRT terminal brand Y, *if* they have the same type of operating system. The "device drivers" within the operating systems of the two machines take care of apparently enormous differences between them. (A device driver is a short program, usually incorporated into the operating system, that handles the access protocols to the peripheral devices, such as the system console, disk drives, printers, and paper tape readers and punches.) The telecommunications program does not have to be concerned with these matters. Consequently, it is a good idea to use system calls for all I/O functions.

The example just given of an assembly-language program does not use system calls for the interface to the modem; instead, it uses direct calls to the I/O port at which the modem is addressable. The reason for this is that there is no direct provision in most operating systems for a modem interface. Hence there is no standard I/O port for the modem, and no standard set of device drivers. The best means of using system calls in this case would be to "fool" the system into behaving as if the modem were one or more other devices. For example, if the process of getting data from the modem were treated as if the modem were a tape reader, and the output to the modem were treated as if it were going to the system tape punch, for which there is a set of system calls, then the program would not need to use direct I/O as was done above. If, however, the system already has a real tape reader or punch, there is obviously going to be an interference problem.

Some Difficulties

The problem with interfacing with operating systems is that they often attach special meanings to certain control characters. This is not serious if the control characters that activate the operating system of the microcomputer never need to be sent to another computer; or if signals coming in from the other computer are never of the type that will cause the local machine to do strange things. Unfortunately, it sometimes happens that the two computer systems in a communications pair use the same control character for different purposes. Consequently, sometimes the characters to be communicated must be carefully isolated from the operating system so that it does not treat them as input from the console and perform undesired functions. Similarly, it may be necessary to filter certain control characters out of the data stream coming in from the modem so that potentially disruptive characters do not get into the system. This is particularly true for characters that may cause the system console, if it is an "intelligent" terminal, to go into unwanted modes of operation. This practice is exemplified by the set of instructions in MODIN (above) that strip out all but a few control characters. These precautions should allow the program to be used with most CP/M-like systems.

A problem with system calls may also come up. If the operating system to be used does not allow direct access to I/O ports, as is the case with some of the UNIX™-like multi-user operating systems, then the program *must* be written using system calls (or their equivalent) throughout. There may be no option in these cases. Such systems may further complicate matters by having I/O buffers as part of their ordinary device drivers and/or special hardware provisions for communications with external devices. In these cases the programmer must take special pains to ensure compatibility with the operating systems. In Cromemco's Cromix™ system, for example, all such I/O must, in practice, be handled through

their IOP (for Input/Output Processor) board, which has its own Z80 microprocessor and memory and can control several I/O boards and attached modems or
other devices. Although this feature substantially increases the cost of the hardware, it also gives the system much greater flexibility and isolates the main
microprocessor from the details of communication.

7

The software presented in the last chapter will allow a microcomputer with modem to operate in a "dumb" terminal mode only. Further, the software is relatively restricted even in that mode of operation. It will not allow the operator to change the baud rate, duplex mode, or parity requirements from the keyboard; the program itself must be changed to accomplish this. In this chapter we are going to see how one might add a variety of different capabilities to the system through appropriate software changes. As was mentioned earlier, the software presented here may not be usable as is by your own system; some modifications may have to be made to tailor it to your own operating system or hardware. Even so, the general procedures to follow are the same for most microcomputers.

A MODULAR PHILOSPHY

One of the most critical things for the programmer to keep in mind when developing telecommunications software, or any other kind for that matter, is that the requirements will invariably change after the "final" design is finished. Therefore it is important to design the software so that it can be improved and expanded at a later date, and with minimum trauma. One of the best ways to do this is through the development of modules in the program. Each module fits within the overall structure and can be worked on independently of the rest of the program. Therefore, when a requirement changes it is a relatively simple matter to change the appropriate module to meet the new conditions; it is not necessary to change the entire software package (although it will be necessary to recompile a previously compiled program.

In the simple communications program of Chapter 6 we had only two modules: initialize interface, and communicate. Now we will expand upon and add to those modules. First, it would be nice, even with a dumb terminal, if we could easily change some of the interface characteristics from the console. All of the basic requirements are already in the program. All we need is some way to change the interface parameters from the keyboard. Next, it would be of great use if we could perform many of the routine microcomputer functions, such as transferring or creating files, performing computations, and the like, while in communications mode. Here we need to add several modules to the communications module, and give ourselves the option of adding more as the need arises. Finally, we want to be sure that control of the use of these modules is in the

Adding Capability

operator's hands, and that exercise of that control is easily done by the operator (that is, the operator-machine interface is "friendly").

In the early days of personal computerdom (way back in the late 1970s) memory was expensive and the overriding concern was that utilities such as the telecommunications programs be of the minimum possible length in order to maintain as much space as possible for "useful" programs and data. These minimum-length utility programs consequently had very terse, often codelike operator interfaces. If you happened to remember the code, all was well. Otherwise, you quickly became confused by the cryptic statements being presented by the computer. Now, with memory considerably cheaper, we can afford to spend more time—and memory—in making the programs understandable.

One of the most popular ways of maintaining a friendly interface is to present the operator with a *menu* of options available at a "branch point" in the program. [A branch point, as the name implies, is a point in the flow of a program where several options are possible for the next set of instructions, one of which must be chosen.] This menu presentation method is very useful for beginning or occasional users of a program. Of course, one of the options for the expert user may be to eliminate the presentation of the menu as an unnecessary frill. In any case, we shall proceed with the development of a set of modules built around a menu-selection concept.

But first, we should decide what modules may be desired in this new, expanded version of the telecommunications program. Figure 7-1 shows some possibilities. We also have included an increased capability for the modem in this case: an originate/answer modem is assumed, one that can both call up another computer to start communications (originate mode) and answer calls from another computer without human intervention (answer mode). This adds a complication to the software and, also, to the microcomputer owner's bank account: The former is expanded in size and complexity; the latter is reduced in size by the high cost of originate/answer modems (compared with that of simple acoustic-coupled or direct-connect originate-only modems).

There are four menus in the program. The first is quite simple. It asks whether the user wishes to operate in the originate or answer mode, or change some of the operating parameters, or receive general information about program operation. The next two menus each deal with the details of the communications in one of the two main modes. Both require that the basic communications parameters, such as baud rate, parity, number of stop bits, and duplex mode, be established, either through the use of default settings or of the fourth menu. Only in the originate mode—and only for some modems—does the program dial a number. The dial-a-number mode may also have a menu if the program is expanded to include a dial-up table of numbers. Both modes must have access to the means for establishing communications with another computer, but here it is gained automatically in the normal program sequence rather than as a result

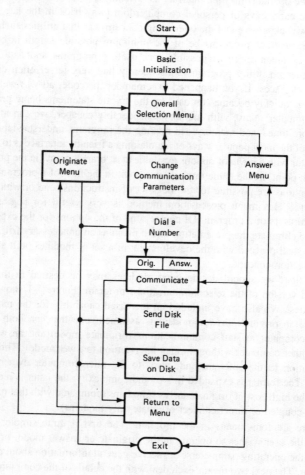

Figure 7-1
General Structure for Advanced Programs

of a menu selection. Finally, both modes should have the ability to send the contents of a disk file to another computer, save data from the other computer on a disk file, return to the previous menu or go to another menu for a different selection, or quit the program altogether.

In the answer mode, the microcomputer is acting as the "host," and so it may be desirable to put some restrictions on what can be transferred to and from disk files so that sensitive or valuable files may be protected from unauthorized access or revision. You may also wish to restrict access to peripheral devices. In this chapter we shall assume that the control over disk-file activity rests with the operator of the host computer, rather than with the person calling in. This type of control requires that the operator be present during transactions involving the answer mode, such as computer teleconferencing situations, and so does not allow for unattended operation of the computer. That is more complicated still, as we shall see later.

ORIGINATE/ANSWER MODEMS

There are a number of originate/answer modems available on the commercial market. Many of these are made for operation with dumb terminals. Consequently they act solely as modems; they only transform the signals from analog to digital or vice versa, and perform no other function. In the simplest of cases the conversion from its originate-only version into an originate/answer modem of this type requires only that a switch be included in the system to reverse the transmission and reception frequency assignments (see Chapter 5). However, this type of modem does not allow for some niceties, such as automatic dialing. There are several modems available that do have these additional features and are specifically designed for use with microcomputers. For the rest of this chapter such a modem will be assumed as the hardware component of the system. Specifically, the instructions used in the following program elements will be those appropriate to one of the D. C. Hayes modems. Other manufacturers will have similar, if not identical, instruction formats.

Physically, the modem consists of two parts. One fits inside the microcomputer, plugging directly into its motherboard or accessory bus, while the other part includes the data access arrangement and interconnecting cables that plug into the telephone line, generally via a modular plug. The dial is replaced by the keyboard of the microcomputer's console.

In order to initialize the modem, certain facts must be known about the registers it uses to communicate with the outside world. These details must be included in the communications program, as some were in the example shown in the last chapter. With an auto-answer modem there are additional registers, as can be seen from the figure. For the D. C. Hayes 80-103A modem the register arrangements are shown in Figure 7-2. Later models and other makes have similar arrangements.

```
---------------------------------------------------------------
                        INPUT REGISTERS

                         Bit Number

DATA REGISTER*   :  7  :  6  :  5  :  4  :  3  :  2  :  1  :  0  :
Address = Base   :DATA :DATA :DATA :DATA :DATA :DATA :DATA :DATA :

STATUS REGISTER  :  7  :  6  : \/  :  4  :  3  :  2  :  1  :  0  :
Address = Base+1 : RI  : CD  : /\  : OE  : FE  : PE  : TRE : RRF :

RRF:  Receiver  Register  Full     1 = Character in the register
TRE:  Transmitter Reg. Empty       1 = Ready to transmit
PE:   Parity Error                 1 = Parity error
FE:   Framing Error                1 = Framing error (see Chap. 5)
OE:   Overflow Error               1 = Data overflow
CD:   Carrier Detect               1 = Carrier detected
RI:   NOT Ring Indicator           0 = Phone is ringing
---------------------------------------------------------------

                       OUTPUT REGISTERS

                         Bit Number

CONTROL REG. 1   : \/  : \/  : \/  :  4  :  3  :  2  :  1  :  0  :
Address = Base+1 : /\  : /\  : /\  : PI  : SBS : LS2 : LS1 : EPE :

EPE:  Even Parity Enable           1 = Even parity
LS1 & LS2: Length Select bits      00 = 5 bits
                                   01 = 6 bits
                                   10 = 7 bits
                                   11 = 9 bits
SBS:  Stop Bit Select              1 = 2 stop bits, 0 = 1 stop bit
PI:   Parity Inhibit               1 = No parity bit

CONTROL REG. 2   :  7  : \/  :  5  :  4  :  3  :  2  :  1  :  0  :
Address = Base+2 : OH  : /\  : RID : ST  : BK  : MS  : TXE : BRS :

BRS:  Bit Rate Select              1 = 300 baud, 0 = 110 baud
TXE:  Transmitter Enable           1 = Carrier on
MS:   Mode Select                  1 = Originate, 0 = Answer
BK:   Break                        1 = Exchange mark and space
ST:   Self Test                    1 = Self test mode
RID:  Ring Indicator Disable       1 = Disable
OH:   Off Hook                     0 = Hang up phone
```

Figure 7-2
I/O Registers for D.C. Hayes 80–103A Modem

INITIALIZATION MODULE

With these additions the initialization part of the program, written in the same dialect of BASIC as the example in Chapter 6, becomes:

```
5     Imode : X=0.1234 : If X>0 Then Run : Set 0,-1
10    Rem The above sets the computer to integer arithmetic mode
15    Rem  -- and resets it if it doesn't work the first time
20    Rem The purpose is to save memory space and slightly increase
25    Rem the speed of execution.
30    Rem  The 'Set' command suppresses the  normal  system limitation
35    Rem on line I/O line length

40    Rem ****************** BASIC Modem Driver ******************
45    Rem
50    Rem This is written in Cromemco 32K Structured BASIC
55    Rem  - other BASICs may have slightly different formats
60    Rem * This program is for use with a D. C. Hayes or similar modem
65    Rem   set at port address C0H (192 decimal)
70    Rem   but may be used with other modems with suitable changes.
```

```
75   Rem  ------------------------------------------------------------
80   Rem                   First Part: Initialization
85   Rem  ------------------------------------------------------------

90   Rem                        ** SET UP **
95   Rem -- First, establish the addresses of the I/O ports:
100  Dataport=%00C0% : Rem The "%" signs enclose hexadecimal numbers
105  Rem The base I/O port address, to which the I/O board is switched,
110  Rem is C0 (hexadecimal). Any other port may be used that is not
115  Rem in conflict with other functions of your computer.
120  Constat=0 : Condata=1 : Rem Console status and data ports
125  Statport=Dataport+1 : Rem This is the modem status register
130  Rem and the D. C. Hayes control register #1 (parity select bits)
135  Modeport=Dataport+2 : Rem This port is for the Hayes control reg. #2
140  Timeport=Dataport+3 : Rem This is the timer in later version Hayes
141  Rem                    modems
145  Rem                    ------------------
150  Sayonara=4 : Rem Control-D; used to terminate the program
152  Transtop=19 : Trango=17 : Rem Control signals to stop or start
153  Rem                                transmission
155  Lfeed=10 : Cret=13 : Rem ASCII value for line feed, carriage return
157  Bel$=Chr$(7) : Rem Console Bell
160  Rem The following are the codes for the Hayes registers
165  Rrf=%0001% : Tre=%0002% : Pe=%0004% : Fe=%0008% : Oe=%0010%
166  Tmr=%0020% : Cd=%0040%
170  Ri=%0080% : Onhook=%007F% : Rem Ring detect: 1 if NOT ringing
175  Epe=%0001% : Ls1=%0002% : Ls2=%0004% : Sbs=%0008% : Pi=%0010%
180  Brs=%0001% : Txe=%0002% : Ms=%0004% : Bk=%0008%
181  St=%0010% : Rid=%0020%
185  Oh=%0080% : Wrdlgth=Ls1+Ls2
190  Wordbyte=Wrdlgth+Pi : Rem Word = 8 data bits, 1 stop bit, no parity
195  Modebyte=Brs : Rem 300 baud default value
200  Dupflag=-1 : Rem This sets the default to full duplex operation
205  Modatardy=Rrf : Condatardy=%0040% : Rem This means that data has
206  Rem                                  been received.
210  Moxmtrdy=Tre : Conxmtrdy=%0080% : Rem When this is true, it's OK
211  Rem                                to send data
215  Clear$=Chr$(27)+"E" : Rem Clear the console screen (Heath/Zenith)
220  Dim Value$(0),Number$(11),Table$(119),Tnumber$(11) : Rem String
221  Rem                                              dimension limits
225  Dim Disk$(0),Fname$(11),File$(13),String$(127) : Rem Disk file data
```

As you can see, most of the initialization process is taken up in defining symbols to be used later, so we do not have to remember all of those binary numbers, and in setting up some default values for the modem operating parameters. Now we can go on to the main parts of the program.

MENU MODULES

The next task in the sequence of events outlined in Figure 7-1 is that of setting up the selection menu. This can be confined to a simple greeting and a request for a selection of one of the secondary menus or program exit, as follows:

```
1000 #MMenu
1002     Repeat
1006     #P1 : Print Clear$ : Print "MICROCOMPUTER TELECOMMUNICATIONS PROGRAM"
1010     Print "Please select one of the following:
1020     Print "1 - Dial up another computer. If a person  answers, hang up"
1030     Print "2 - Wait for a call from another computer"
1035     Print "3 - Change the communication parameters"
1040     Print "4 - Exit the program"
1050     Print: Print: Input "Which do you select? ",Choice
1060     If Choice<=1 Or Choice>=4 Then Goto P1
1070     If Choice=1 Then Call .Originate
1075     If Choice=2 Then Call .Answer
1080     If Choice=3 Then Call .Changer
1085     If Choice=4 Then Do
```

```
1086 Rem The following is used if you want to confine use to this program
1087      Noecho:  Input "Enter the password ",Pass$ : Rem Noecho suppresses
1088      Rem                                      display of the password
1089      Echo:  If Pass$="1234567" Then Choice=5
1090      Else
1092      Choice=0
1094      Enddo
1096   Until Choice=5 : Rem The bad password gets the runaround
1097 Stop
1098 End

1100 Procedure .Originate : Rem Originate mode procedure starts here
     .
     .
     .
1200 Procedure .Answer : Rem Answer mode procedure starts here
     .
     .
     .
1300 Procedure .Changer : Rem Parameter changing procedure starts here
     .
     .
     .
```

This short program constitutes the module containing the rest of the program contents as a series of CALLs to procedures. Each procedure is essentially self-contained and is designed so that it can be lifted out and used in other programs. This use of procedures is common to structured languages but is relatively infrequent in BASIC dialects. Note that the name of the procedure is preceded by a '.' in the Cromemco dialect. Each of the procedures has its own menu.

Originate Procedure

The originate menu might look something like this:

```
1100 Procedure .Originate
1102 Repeat
1106  Print Clear$ : Rem Originate mode menu

1110 *Omenu : Ms=4 : Print "ORIGINATE MODE" : Print
1115     Repeat
1120     Print "You may select any one of the following:"
1125     Print "1 - Dial another computer"
1130     Print "2 - Send a file to the other computer"
1135     Print "3 - Save this transaction on a disk file"
1140     Print "4 - Disconnect an existing call"
1150     Print "5 - Go to the main menu": Print
1160     Input "Now, which do you select? ", Origsel
1165     If Origsel=1 Then Do
1166       If Commflag=1 Then Do
1167         Print "You're already connected!" : Origsel=0
1168       Else
1169         Gosub Dialer
1170       Enddo
1171     Enddo
1172     While Origsel>1 And Origsel<5
1175     On (Origsel-1) Gosub Sender,Saver,Ender
1180     Endwhile
1185   Until Origsel = 5
1190  Choice=0
1195  Exitproc
```

In this module there are also some features not common to all BASIC programs, such as the use of subroutine labels instead of line numbers (for example, "Dialer"). Notice also that there is some fancy flag keeping in lines 1166–1170 to keep from interrupting an existing call.

The answer-mode module is similar in appearance to the originate-mode module except that it does not contain the dialing option. All three of the main menu modules should also have statements to deal with selections other than those listed in the menus, that is, input errors or special functions available only to "those in the know."

Programming Tip: To avoid hours of frantic debugging of mysterious ailments, build up and test the program one module at a time.

OPERATIONS MODULES

This section includes one example each of procedures and subroutines (notice that the previous menus could have been set up to use either).

Changing Communications Parameters

The simplest of the operations modules is the one that changes the communications parameters. This module asks for changes in the parameters, one by one. Alternatively, it may present a menu of options and ask the operator to select one parameter to be changed, change it, then ask for another or an exit command. As an example, consider the following:

```
1300 Procedure .Changer : Rem Change the communications parameters
1301   Print Clear$
1305   Print "Please enter a new value for those parameters you"
1310   Print "wish to change.  If no change is required, press"
1315   Print "   RETURN.  To exit press ESC" : Print : Print
1317   On Esc Goto Final
1320   Print "          TABLE OF PARAMETERS"
1325   Print "Bit Rate:  0 = 110 Baud, 1 = 300 Baud"
1330   Print "Word Length:  0 = 5 bits, 2 = 6 bits, 4 = 7 bits, 6 = 8 bits"
1335   Print "Parity inhibit = 16, enable = 0"
1340   Print "If parity is enabled, then Even parity = 1, odd = 0"
1345   Print "One stop bit = 0, two stop bits = 8"
1347   Print "Full duplex = -1, Half duplex = 0 : Print
1350   Print "Enter the new bit rate [";Brs;"]"; : Input" >",Value$
1355   If Value$ <>"" Then Brs = Binand(Val(Value$),1)
1360   Print "Enter the new word length [";Wrdlgth;"]": Input" >",Value$
1362   If Value$<>"" Then Do
1365      Value = 2*Int(Val(Value$)/2.0) : Rem even numbers only
1370      If (Value >=0 And Value <=6) Then Wrdlgth=Value
1372   Enddo
1375   Print "Enter the parity inhibit bit [";Pi;"]"; : Input" >",Value$
1380   If Value$ <>"" Then Pi= Binand(Val(Value$),%0010%)
1385      While Pi=0
1390      Print "Even or odd parity? [";Epe;"]"; : Input" >",Value$
1395      If Value$ <>"" Then Epe = Binand(Val(Value$),1)
1400      Endwhile
1405   Print "Enter the number of stop bits [";Sbs;"]";
1410   Input" >",Value$
1415   If Value$ <>"" Then Sbs = Binand(Val(Value$),8)
1420   Print "Finally, enter the duplex mode [";Dupflag;"]";
1425   Input " >",Value$
1430   If Value$ <>"" Then Dupflag=Binand(Val(Value$),%00FF%)
1435   Modebyte=Brs : Wordbyte=Wrdlgth+Sbs+Pi
1440   Choice=0
1450  *Final : Endproc
```

The previous **Binand(A,B)** function performs a logical *AND* operation with the two arguments (A and B) of the function. This is a way of ensuring that only the intended bits get changed. For example an input error of 5 in the word length selection would result in a 7-bit word and no change in parity. If no such safeguard were employed the parity could be set to even, whether or not the operator intended it that way.

Another useful, friendly device is the inclusion of an escape mode in case the operator really didn't want to change anything, or anything else, after all. This is not mandatory, just another one of those memory-requirement-increasing features that makes the program more comfortable to work with.

Note that the parameter-changing mode always interconnects with the main selection menu since it is called, via the menu, from other modules.

Automatic Dialing

The next step in the sequence is more complicated. Here the program must accept a telephone number from the console or fetch a number from a prestored list, take the "telephone off the hook," wait for a dial tone, generate the dialing pulses, wait for an answer, if any, and then hand over to the connect module. This process is diagrammed in Figure 7-3.

The key complication in this module is the introduction of some fairly precise timing considerations. If the modem itself doesn't have a built-in timer that is accessible to the program, then the program must generate its own timing loops. In the later versions of the D. C. Hayes modems, for example, there is a 50-millisecond timer (0.050, or one-twentieth, of a second) that is controlled by an additional output register, control register #3. Any bit sent to that register will start the timer. The timer status is given by bit 5 of the status register. For the following example we are taking the easy route by assuming that the modem has a 50-ms. (millisecond, or thousandth of a second) timer.

```
1500 *Dialer : Rem This module dials a phone number
1505   Print Clear$ : Print "Do you wish to enter a number to be dialed (D)"
1510   Input "or do you wish to use the table (T)? ",Value$
1515   If Value$ = "D" Or Value$ = "d" Then Do
1520      Print "Enter the number to be dialed.  Do NOT use parentheses"
1525      Print "or dashes to separate parts of the number."
1530      Input Number$
1540      Else
1550      Print "Which of the following numbers do you want dialed?"
1560      Print "1 - Local SOURCE number"
1565      Print "2 - Local CompuServe number"
1570      Print "3 - University Computer service"
  .       Print    . . .
  .          .
  .          .
1595   Rem the following table comprises a sequence of 12 digit numbers of the
1596   Rem form 9-1-xxx-xxx-xxxx, where the dashes are left out and the 9 (for
1597   Rem reaching an outside line) and 1 (for long distance) prefixes may be
1598   Rem replaced by blanks.  The first set of x's is the area code, etc.
1600   Table$="   2135551234918055555......."
1602   J=0 : Rem Probably not required, but just to make sure
1605   Rem The number to be dialed is picked from the string next
1610   Input Numr : Tnumber$=Table$(12*(Numr-1),12*Numr-1)
1611      For I= 0 To 11
1612      If Number$(I,I)=" " Then Next I
```

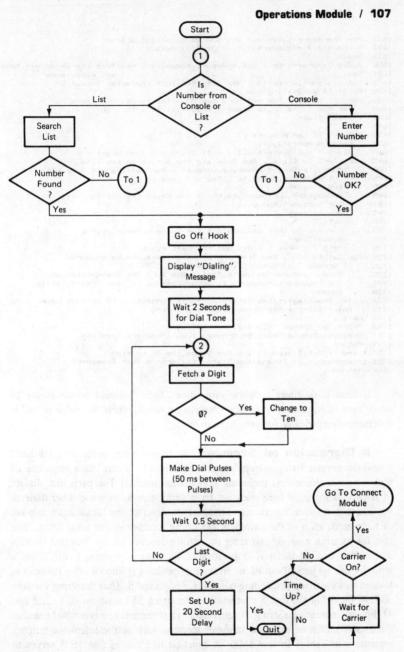

Figure 7-3
Diagram of Automatic Dialing Module

```
1613  Rem The above takes out any spaces by skipping them
1615  Number$(J,J)=Tnumber$(I,I) : J=J+1 : Next I
1618  Enddo
1620  Modebyte=Brs+Ms+Oh : Out Modeport,Modebyte : Rem Take the phone off hook,
1621  Rem                                          set rate, mode
1622  Out Statport,Wordbyte : Rem Get the right character format
1625  Print "I am Dialing now ---"
1630  For I=1 to 40 : Rem Set up 2 second delay to get dial tone
1635    Rem Start the 50 ms timer & wait 'til it's through
1640    Gosub Timer
1645  Next I
1650  For I=0 To Len(Number$)-1
1655    Print Number$(I,I);
1660    Digit = Val(Number$(I,I)) : If Digit = 0 Then Digit = 10
1665    For J=1 To Digit : Rem Generate the pulses on the line
1670      Modebyte=Binand(Modebyte,Onhook) : Rem Set the off hook bit
1675      Out Modeport,Modebyte : Rem and send it
1680      Gosub Timer
1685      Modebyte=Binor(Modebyte,Oh) : Rem Reset the off hook bit
1687      Out Modeport,Modebyte
1690      Gosub Timer
1700    Next J
1705    For J=1 To 10 : Rem Now get the space between digits
1710      Gosub Timer
1720    Next J : Next I : Rem Get the next digit
1725  For I=1 to 600 : Rem Give the phone 30 secs. to be answered
1730    If Binand(Inp(Statport),Cd) Then Do
1732      Modebyte=Binor(Modebyte,Txe) : Ren Turn the transmitter on
1734      Out Modeport,Modebyte : Gosub Commune : Rem Begin talking
1736    Enddo
1737    If Commflag=1 Then Return : Rem If connection is already made, stop
1738    Gosub Timer : Rem Otherwise, keep trying
1740  Next I
1745  Print "No Answer!";Chr$(7) : Commflag=0
1747  Modebyte=Binand(Modebyte,Onhook) : Out Modeport,Modebyte
1749  Return
1750  *Timer : Out Timeport,-1 : Rem Start the 50 ms timer
1755  *Timecheck : If Binand(Inp(Statport),Tmr)= 0 Then Timecheck
1760  Return
```

If there is no timer then the subroutine "Timer" should do something to waste time like adding two numbers together n times, where the value of "n" is determined empirically for your system.

A Digression on Strings: The program segments thus far have contained several string-manipulation functions. (A "string" is a sequence of alphanumeric characters, including punctuation marks.) The particular dialect of BASIC being used here does not have string arrays, as some other dialects do. There is no such function as String$(I) to describe the Ith stringlet in a set of n. Instead, all n of the stringlets are strung together in one long string. The rule for locating a single character in a string depends on the fact that (in this dialect) the first character is in position 0, the next in position 1, etc. Thus a stringlet can be picked out of an array if its position is known. The stringlet is located by its starting and ending positions, say, m and n. Thus the string variable S$(0,4) picks out the first 5 characters in the string S$ (positions 0, 1, 2, 3 and 4). For use in treating a string as equivalent to a string array, this method requires the establishment of standard stringlet lengths, such as the telephone-number sequences in Table$ in line 1600. A function like that of line 1605 serves to pick out individual strings once their relative position in the "table" is known. The remainder of the routine makes the connection and gets ready for the subsequent interactive communications.

COMMUNICATION MODULE

After all of this the computer is at last ready to get down to the basics of actually communicating with the other machine. This is where we were at about line 250 of the program in Chapter 6!

We can use the program segment of Chapter 6 for the communications sequence, with just a few additions and modifications. One of the additions is a check for a command to go to one of the menus so that we may make use of other options such as sending disk files or saving incoming text. We also may want to send special control characters to the other computer. These should be included in the menu of allowed possibilities for transmission. The program in Chapter 6 and the following example both allow all characters to be sent *from* the console but only some to be sent *to* the console. If we are in the answer mode we may wish to operate in full-duplex, that is, echo all incoming characters except those special control characters. We may also want to modify the list of "bad" characters. The following listing shows the main routine and subroutines of Chapter 6 with some likely additions and/or modifications marked in boldface.

```
2000  #Commune
2001    Print"Go ahead, please --- Control-D will switch you to the main menu"
2002    Print Chr$(7)
2005    Noesc : Rem This stops automatic checking of the console
2010    Commflag=1 : Rem Note that communication has begun
2015    Repeat
2020    Rem First check the console status and also for an ABORT signal
2021    Rem  from the console
2025      While Binand(Inp(Constat),Condatardy) And Not Quitflag
2050        Gosub Consproc : Rem If the console has a byte, process it
2055      Endwhile : Rem End of the console loop
2060      While Binand(Inp(Statport),Modatardy) : Rem check the modem status
2065        Gosub Modemproc : Rem If there is a byte, process it
2070      Endwhile : Rem End of the modem loop
2075    Until Quitflag
2080    Esc : Rem This turns the automatic console checking back on
2085    Return
2090    Rem --------------------------------------------------------------------
2095  #Consproc : Rem This routine processes ASCII characters from the console
2100    Character=Inp(1) : Rem Get the character from the console data port
2105    Character=Binand(Character,%007F%) : Rem Set the parity bit to 0
2110    If Character=Sayonara Then Quitflag=-1 : Return : Rem Stop char. received
2115    If Character=Lfeed Then Return : Rem Don't send a line feed to the modem
2120    Rem Wait until the modem is ready for the character
2125  #Modcheck : If Binand(Inp(Statport),Moxatrdy)=0 Then Goto Modcheck
2130    Out Dataport,Character : Rem Send the character to the modem
2135    If Dupflag Then Return : Rem Don't echo the character if full-duplex
2140    Print Chr$(Character); : Rem Otherwise echo it to the console
2142    If Saveflag=1 Then String$(Csave,Csave)=Character : Csave=Csave+1 : Rem Us
ed in file save mode
2145    If Character=13 Then Print : Rem Add a line feed if it was a CR
2150    Return
2155    Rem ----------------------------------------------------
2160  #Modemproc : Rem This routine processes ASCII characters from the modem
2165    Character=Inp(Dataport) : Rem Get the character from the modem
2170    Character=Binand(Character,%007F%) : Rem Strip the parity bit
2175    Badflag=0 : Gosub Badchar : Rem Check for banned characters
2180    If Badflag Then Return : Rem Ignore the bad guys
2185    Print Chr$(Character); : Rem Otherwise display it
2187    If Binand(Modebyte,Ma)=0 Then Gosub Modcheck : Rem Echo if in answer mode
2188    If Saveflag=1 Then String$(Csave,Csave)=Character : Csave=Csave+1
2189    Rem The above is used in file save mode
2190    Return
2195    Rem            ####
2200  #Badchar : Rem This routine checks for undesirable characters
2205    Rem This should be customized to your particular system
```

```
2210  Rem The following rejects only Control- characters other than
2215  Rem BEL,BS,HT,LF,VT,FF, CR, DEL and ESCape
2220  If Character>31 And Character<128 Then Return : Rem Print all letters,
2221  Rem                                              numbers, etc.
2225  If Character<7 Then Badflag=-1 : Return
2230  If Character>13 And Character<27 Then Badflag=-1 : Return
2235  If Character>27 Then Badflag=-1
2240  Return
```

At this point the accumulated program performs essentially the same functions that the acoustic-coupler modem program did in Chapter 6, with the notable exception that the present program automatically dials phone numbers and can change communication parameters in mid-stream. The main innovation to be added is the ability to transfer disk files.

TRANSFERRING FILES

File transfer is one of the most important features to be added to a communicating microcomputer system. With this capability a considerable amount of flexibility is added, flexibility that allows considerably greater diversity of operation of the system. In principle, the files to be transferred can be almost anything: text, data bases, programs, messages, graphics, whatever can be stored in digital form. In practice, there may be some additional difficulties to be overcome.

Limitations

HARDWARE. The first of these difficulties has to do with hardware limitations. It is a relatively simple task to open a disk file on the host microcomputer and send it out to the computer at the other end of the telecommunications link without interruption. However, it is more difficult, and perhaps even impractical, to receive a stream of text, save it temporarily in memory, and transfer it to a disk file without interruption.

The reason for this is that most contemporary microcomputer systems have only a single CPU, and it must handle *all* of the data manipulation of the system, including all I/O processes. In the case where the tasks of the CPU include intercepting all data coming in from the modem port, saving it in memory, reading a portion of memory into a disk file, and handling all of the disk-control operations, it's no wonder that occasionally the CPU drops one of the balls it's trying to juggle.

The first aspect of this problem that must be addressed is that of available space in the memory for storing the incoming data. Clearly, the more storage space there is, the better off the communicator is. If the available storage space is always larger than the size of any files to be recorded, then the problem of trying to transfer from memory to disk while also transferring from modem to memory goes away. The microcomputer can concern itself simply with accepting the incoming data, and then tuck it away somewhere on a disk at a later, calmer time. This is what many commercially available communications programs do:

they limit the size of the interceptable file to the size of the fast memory available to the microcomputer.

PROGRAM SIZE. This problem is also the basis for another fundamental type of decision: the language in which the communications program is written. The preceding material has been presented primarily in a BASIC interpreter (or compiler-interpreter) that, together with the source code for the communications program, takes up large amounts of space, as we have seen. It is a much better idea to have the final communications program written in assembler, or in another compact-code-producing language such as FORTH or C, so that the maximum possible space in fast memory is left for storage of incoming data files.

PROTOCOLS. Even with this precaution, however, there will likely come a time when you will wish to transfer a file that is larger than the space available in the memory of your microcomputer. In this case it is necessary to have some means of signalling the computer sending the data to stop transmitting while your poor, overworked CPU transfers the information to a disk file. If the incoming data stream does not stop during this process it is quite possible that data will be lost. You will be able to confirm this by noting the overflow signal coming from the modem's UART, but this is small consolation for the arduous process of recovering the lost data (which is sometimes not even possible). Therefore, some form of "handshaking" procedure is called for in the data transmission/reception programs in both computers.

In the program as provided thus far, two control signals for this handshaking operation are included: Control-S and Control-Q (or "Transtop" and "Trango," as they are labelled in the program). If both computers engaged in the communication recognize these signals as commands to stop or resume transmission, then the data transfer operation might proceed quite smoothly; the next complication would not occur until the disk ran out of space. Unfortunately, smoothness of transmission is not guaranteed even in this situation.

For example, suppose that the computer at the other end transmits data by filling a buffer with, say, 128 bytes. It then sends out those 128 bytes without bothering to listen for any cries of distress from your end. If you run out of memory in the middle of one of those 128-byte bursts then your immediate transmission of a control-S upon fillup falls upon deaf transistors. Many computers operate that way because stopping to listen for a gripe after each character transmitted slows down the data rate too much for most purposes. After all, most minicomputers and mainframes operate under the assumption that they are communicating with a dumb terminal having no provision for file transfer. The designers of the communication software for these machines consider the 300 baud is already too slow for efficient data transfer; it is not to be slowed further for error checking. In short, unless you are communicating with another computer that uses identical communications software, you may run into problems in transferring long files to your microcomputer.

LANGUAGE STANDARDS. This is an aspect of a problem frequently mentioned in this book and in most others that delve into the details of hardware or software: standards. The BASIC language is particularly afflicted with dialects. The areas of disagreement among dialects of a language tend to concentrate in the Input/Output handling insturctions, which is what we are concerned with at the moment. Different systems have different I/O commands. Thus this area of a "standard" program in BASIC is often the one most changed as the program migrates to different computer systems. This problem is another reason for writing the program in assembly language, either from the start or after the program has been tested; compiled assembly-language problems are understood by all CPUs of the same variety (that is, all Z80s understand Z80 programs, all 6502s understand 6502 programs, etc.).

OPERATING SYSTEM STANDARDS. Finally, as mentioned earlier, there are problems produced by differences in operating systems. Instructions that involve standard system calls in one operating system may find them unavailable, or may even conflict with calls, in another operating system. This is not a problem in the data communications process itself, since the communications software will be tailored to the operating system in use. It is a problem in *portability* of the software. A program that works on system A may be useless on system B even if both use the same type of CPU. CDOS℠, the operating system assumed for the examples shown here, is similar to, but not identical with, the later versions of CP/M℠. Thus the reader must make sure, in adapting the ideas presented here to another system, to take note of these issues of translation.

The Transmission Process

With that out of the way, let us consider two example disk-transfer program modules. First, the easy one: sending a file to another computer. In a mood of caution, this program keeps checking for a Control-S from the other computer. If it gets one, it stops transmission until a Control-Q is received, whereupon it resumes sending the file. Other control characters may be substituted for these, as appropriate to the computer with which you are communicating.

```
3000  $Sender : Print Clear$ : Rem Disk file transmission module
3002  On Esc Stop
3005  Rem First get the file name
3010  Print "Enter the name of the file you wish transmitted"
3015  $Help : Print "If you do not know the file name, press ESC to temporarily"
3020  Print "exit the program, type "DIR <CR>" to get the disk directory,"
3025  Input "then type "CON <CR>" to continue the program.",Dummy$
3030  On error goto Help
3035  Input "File name? >",Fname$
3040  Input "On what drive is the file? ",Disk$
3045  File$=Disk$+":"+Fname$ : Rem Concatenates parts to get file name
3046  Rem                             in form d:file.ext
3050  On error Goto Error'handler
3055  Open\1,128\File$ : Rem Opens a file in channel 1 and accepts 128 byte
3060  Rem                       long pieces of the file - this is the standard
3065  Rem                       record length in CDOS(tm) and CP/M(tm).
3070  Rec=0 : Eof=0 : Goflag=-1 : Rem Set to first record, not end-of-file
```

```
3075    Repeat
3080    Get\1,Rec\String$ : Get a record from the disk
3085    For I=0 To 127 : Rem Send it out and display it
3090       Character=Asc(String$(I,I) : Rem Get the next character in ASCII form
3095    #Modout : If Binand(Inp(Statport),Maxmtrdy)=0 Then Goto Modout
3100       Out Dataport,Character : Rem Send the character to the modem
3105       Print String$(I,I); : Rem Echo it to the console
3110    #Modin : If Binand(Statport,Rrf) Then Do : Rem If the modem has
3111       Rem                                  a char., fetch it
3115       Character=Inp(Dataport) : Rem Get the character from the modem
3120       Character=Binand(Character,%007F%) : Rem Strip the parity bit
3125       If Character=Transtop Then Goflag=0 : Rem Quit transmitting
3130       If Character=Trango Then Goflag=-1 : Rem    until a go-ahead
3135       Enddo
3140    If Not Goflag Then Goto Modin
3145    Next I
3150    #Lastrec
3155    Until Eof
3160    Print "File Sent";Chr$(7) : Close : Rem Close the file and finish
3165    Return
3200    Rem ----------------------------------------------------------------
3500    #Error'handler
3505    Rem The following instruction traps file name errors and returns
3510    If Sys(3)=128 Then Print "NO SUCH FILE";Chr$(7) : Goto Help
3515    Rem The next instruction traps end-of-file errors
3520    If Sys(3)=138 Then Eof=-1 : Goto Lastrec
3525    Print "HELP! Call an expert!";Chr$(7) : Stop : Rem Other kinds of errors n
eed more analysis
```

Another Digression on Strings: A string variable, such as String$, is "dimensioned" (the software will ignore parts of a string that are longer than the stated dimension) to establish the size explicitly at the beginning of the program. Therefore the statement **Dim String$(127)** in line 225 of the program sets the maximum (and nominal) string length at 128 (positions 0 through 127). A one-character string, such as the identification of the disk drive by Disk$, is dimensioned as Disk$(0)—the string occupies the 0 position only. The length 128 was picked for the standard text string, String$, because this is the size of a standard record on a single-density CDOS™ or CP/M™ disk. Since all disk read and write operations (for those two operating systems, among others) are on the basis of single records, this selection makes for greatest efficiency and minimizes confusion.

The Reception Process

As you recall, from all the caveats mentioned earlier, receiving a file unscathed is trickier than sending it, if only because the computer on the other end is likely to be unconcerned about any problems you might have in capturing the information. It was probably programmed on the assumption that you are not going to store the information except, possibly, via a printing terminal. Hence, we shall investigate two ways of writing a reception module. The first takes no chances. It limits the size of the file it can receive to the fast memory available. This approach naturally places a premium on the compactness of an assembly language or similar compiled program. Nevertheless, we shall illustrate the concept in BASIC.

```
4000 *Saver :   Print Clear$ : Rem Module to save incoming text on disk
4005   Csave=0 : Rem This part sets up the disk save
4010   Memax=Fre(1) : Rem This function gives the amount of available memory
4015   Print "You have space available for ";Memax;" characters. In what file"
4020   Input "do you wish to save the information? ",Fname$
4025   Input "On which drive should the file be located? ",Disk$
4030   File$=Disk$+":"+Fname$
4035   On Error Goto In'errors
4037   Create File$ : Rem Create the SAVE file
4040   Open\1,Memax\File$ : Rem Note that, in this dialect of BASIC
4045   Rem                   the record size is limited to 32,767 characters
4050   Dim String$(Memax-1) : Rem This sets up the accepting string
4055   Print "Control-D will terminate the SAVE process"
4060     Repeat : Rem The following moves the communications loop to here
4065       While Binand(Inp(Constat),Condatardy) And Csave<Memax
                                                   And Csave<Memax
4070       Gosub Consproc : Rem If the console has a byte this processes it
4080       Endwhile : Rem End of the console loop
4085       While Binand(Inp(Statport),Modatardy) And Csave<Memax
4090       Gosub Modemproc : Rem If there is a byte, process it
4095       Csave=Csave+1 : Rem Keep track of the space available
4100       Endwhile : Rem End of the modem loop
4105     Until Quitflag Or Csave=Memax-1
4110   Put\1,0\String$ : Close : Rem Save the text and close the file
4115   Dim String$(127) : Return : Rem Restore String$ to its standard size
4500 *In'errors : File error handling
4505   If Sys(3)=137 Then Do
4510     Print "The file already exists.  Do you wish to overwrite it?"
4520     Input Answer$
4525     If Answer$(0,0)="Y" Or Answer$(0,0)="y" Then Do
4530       Goto 4040
4535     Enddo
4540     Else
4545       Goto 4015
4550   Enddo
```

The more adventurous way of writing this module assumes that the computer on the other end of the line has instantaneous reactions to your start and stop commands. The difference between that approach and the one just shown is:

1. Only a small amount of fast memory is needed; typically just enough to store one disk record's worth of information.

2. The receiver computer keeps sending out Stop and Go signals to the transmitting receiver. A Stop is sent when a record is filled, just prior to saving it on disk. A Go is sent when the record has been saved.

This can be done with just a few added instructions. The revised version of the module looks like this:

```
4000 *Saver :   Print Clear$ : Saveflag=1 : Rem Module to save text on disk
4020   Input "In what file do you wish to save the information? ",Fname$
4025   Input "On which drive should the file be located? ",Disk$
4030   File$=Disk$+":"+Fname$
4035   On Error Goto In'errors : Create File$ : Rem Create the SAVE file
4040   Open\1,128\File$ : Rem The record size should be the standard
4041                          for the operating system
4055   Print "Control-D will terminate the SAVE process"
4060     Repeat : Rem The following moves the communications loop to here
4062     Csave=0 : Rem Set the pointer to the first character in the record
4063       Repeat : Rem This follows the communication, one record at a time
4065         While Binand(Inp(Constat),Condatardy) And Not Quitflag
                                                     And Csave<128
4070         Gosub Consproc : Rem If the console has a byte this processes it
4080         Endwhile : Rem End of the console loop
4085         While Binand(Inp(Statport),Modatardy) And Csave<128
```

```
4090        Gosub Modemproc : Rem If there is a byte, process it
4095        Csave=Csave+1
4100        Endwhile : Rem End of the record packing loop
4105      Until Quitflag Or Csave=128
4106    Character=Transtop : Gosub Modcheck : Rem Blow the whistle
4107    Put\1,Rec\String$ : Rem Save the record
4108    Get\1,Rec\String$ : Rec=Rec+1 : Rem Make sure it's been saved
4109    Character=Trango : Gosub Modcheck : Rem OK to proceed
4110    Until Quitflag
4111  Close : Rem Close the file to be saved
4115  Saveflag =0 : Return
```

ENDING COMMUNICATION

The only part of the program that is left at this juncture is the section labelled Ender. This module takes care of such housekeeping matters as shutting off the transmitter and putting the modem back on hook in a reverse procedure to that of the dialup routine. It then causes control to jump back to the operating system, the BASIC interpreter, or whatever it is configured to do.

With this set of modules the communicating microcomputer has a wide range of possibilities for activities in which it can engage. The next two chapters will describe some of these possibilities, either in terms of the package given above, as is or with some further additions or modifications, or in terms of similar packages.

ADDITIONAL HINTS CONCERNING THOSE OTHER COMPUTERS

With computers running timesharing systems such as IBM's TSO or WYLBUR there may be some further difficulties in using the full array of capabilities described here. First, make sure that the parity of your transmitted signals is acceptable by the other machine. Mark parity (or two stop bits, which is the equivalent) will be accepted by most; other types may not work.

The next problem is that systems such as the two just named may not listen for your computer's frantic STOP cries while they are transmitting files to you. Check this before you depend on this mode for transmission of vital data.

These IBM-based systems also are accustomed to interacting with typewriter-like dumb terminals. Therefore they expect your end to pause for a few moments—a few tenths of a second—after each carriage return. If you are sending a text file to one of these systems it is wise to put in an additional delay after each carriage return sent, so as not to shock the other system's sensibilities (and lose some of your data).

I am not really picking on IBM systems here. The problem is that many large mainframes in operation today just happen to be IBM machines with some of the idiosyncracies just described.

8

The telecommunications programs discussed in the previous chapter will provide basic communications and file transfer capabilities to the microcomputer user. They will satisfy many of the needs for telecommunications capability of the typical microcomputer installation. That is, they will provide those capabilities *if* the missing parts are filled in by the reader, *if* the microcomputer understands Cromemco Structured Basic (or the reader has modified the program to suit the dialect of BASIC that the microcomputer understands), and *if* the microcomputer has enough memory to hold the program, the BASIC interpreter, and any data files that might be transmitted to the machine.

The latter point is particularly important. The version of the "built-in modem" program appearing in Chapter 7 includes a large number of annotations in order to help the reader understand the logic of the program flow and the purpose of each instruction. This annotation is intended to ease the task of translating the program into another dialect of BASIC or into another language altogether, but it makes the program too large to fit into the memory of a microcomputer with a mere 64K of RAM available. To be more precise, the program itself will fit, since it is only 16K bytes long; unfortunately, when the operating system and the compiler/interpreter are added, and the space for storage of variables is included, the total memory requirement exceeds the capacity of most 8-bit microcomputer systems.

These constraints do not make our task hopeless. The first means of easing the pressure is to delete all of the remarks in the operating program since, in most BASIC dialects, the remarks keep occupying space even though they are not used in the execution of the program. The hazard of this is that it may be more difficult for the original programmer (or *a fortiori* another programmer) to change elements of the program later, because the unremarked program is more difficult to understand, as was mentioned earlier. Nonetheless, eliminating the remarks in the version given in the last chapter reduces the program size by almost 50%.

A second means of reducing the amount of space the program occupies is to break it up into separate program modules. In this mode, each major component of the program, such as the initializer, the dialer, the communications module, etc., becomes a separate program called by the main menu. Thus, the branches from the main menu would become a series of RUN statements instead of procedure calls. Each module would RUN the main menu program upon com-

Further Expansion of Software

pletion of its tasks. In this way the system RAM need contain only a small portion of the program at any one time. The tradeoff in this case is that there must now be a disk access (assuming that the programs are stored on a floppy or hard disk) to load each module. This is probably a trivial delay in most circumstances but might be important in some cases.

The third, and most highly recommended, means of shortening the program is, of course, to write it in something approaching assembly language. The program of Chapter 7 occupies about 3K of memory when written in Z80 or 8080 assembler as a command file (*.COM for those familiar with CP/M™ and its variants). No space is required for anything other than the operating system in this mode. Assembly language compilers (or assemblers) automatically eliminate all of the remarks that are included in the *source code* when they produce the file that does the work. The difference is that the source code file—the file containing all of the explanatory remarks—is still available to the programmer at improvement time. In a BASIC file that has had all of the Rem lines deleted the chances are that the remarks will be lost, or at least dissociated from the file, at an early stage. Bewilderment ensues.

To a large extent the issue of assembly language versus BASIC is a transitory one, dependent mainly on the relative costs and capabilities of contemporary microelectronics. In the early 1980s 64K of RAM is relatively expensive, accounting for up to 40% of the cost of a typical microcomputer. Further, the technology of the most popular 8-bit microprocessors limits the size of the memory "page" that can be addressed conveniently to 64K. The consequence is that much time and effort must be spent on minimizing the space occupied by such utility programs as telecommunications controllers so that memory is still available for the results of operation of those programs—the data that are the real interest of the operator of the program. Further, this space problem becomes even more critical when we add the extra, "user-friendly" features discussed in Chapter 4. For these reasons I recommend that a useful telecommunications program for a memory-limited system be written in assembler or in a high-level optimizing compiler.

As the 1980s wear on, these system constraints will swiftly disappear. Continuously addressable memories in the million-byte range will become practical and economical as 256K RAM chips become abundant in the mid-1980s. Microprocessors with 16- and 32-bit words will be common; they will be able to access these larger memories directly, without the constraints of 64K segmentation. Consequently, it will be less of a penalty to use languages such as BASIC to construct utility programs. In the meantime, it is still a problem.

With this future in mind, we can look at some of the additional capabilities that may be desirable for your telecommunications program; capabilities beyond the "basic black" just covered.

FILE TRANSFER OPTIONS IN A NOISY WORLD

As mentioned in the previous chapter, some difficulties may lie in the way of achieving error-free transmission of a file from one computer to another. These difficulties can arise from the operation of either one of the computers, or from the communication line connecting them. The most likely source of errors is the telephone line interconnecting the computers (if that is what is being used as the transmission medium). In a typical switched-line system, the type most microcomputers will use, noise pulses lasting .01 second or so are not unheard of. This does not sound like much to the person listening to a telephone conversation; the sound is a brief click or tick, barely noticeable. In a 300-baud data stream, however, the click wipes out 3 bits, and would generally cause one character in an ASCII data stream to be misinterpreted. One wrong character may not be a crucial error, especially if it can be corrected by inference from its context. However, by the law of the general perversity of nature, noise tends to occur in bursts. Like the proverbial little girl with the curl, transmission can be largely error-free for a long time, then become absolutely horrid. Many characters in a section of text or data can become scrambled by such noise, and the text may become unrecoverable.

There are three common approaches to remedying this situation. They can be summarized as follows:

1. Ignore the problem.
2. Keep a general eye on the process.
3. Watch—and correct—everything.

Naturally, the speed of transmission of a file tends to be inversely related to the amount of care that is taken to prevent errors. The transmission module in Chapter 7 is a minimal version of the second level of error prevention. The transmitting computer simply stops the process when the receiving machine tells it to—for reasons that may have nothing to do with errors in transmission. The following are some of the techniques, advantages, and disadvantages of each of the three options.

Press On Regardless

This method, while laudable in a heroic cavalry charge, and inevitable in some half-duplex systems, does have the greatest capacity among the three for introduction of errors. The process is easily completed by eliminating the **Modin** subroutine (lines 3110 through 3130 and line 3140) from the transmission module of Chapter 7. The sending computer then will send the data to the modem for transmission, regardless of the condition of the transmission line and/or the computer at the other end. This method is clearly the fastest means of data transmission; absolutely nothing gets in the way of the data stream. If there is nothing wrong with either the transmission line or the computer at the receiving end, then it is an excellent option. A good example of a situation in which it might be perfectly acceptable is the transmission of short files (that is, short enough so that no disk accesses have to be made by the receiving computer during file reception) over a hard-wired communications link (two computers interconnected by a cable).

As mentioned earlier, this option may be inevitable when the receiving computer cannot, or is set not to, return an indication concerning the state of the transmission process, and so the only information available to the sending computer is that the communications carrier is still running. Even in this situation it may pay for the programmer of the sending computer to know a little more about the operation of the receiving computer. For instance, as mentioned in the previous chapter, mainframe computers that are programmed in the expectation that they will be connected to typewriter-like terminals also expect a certain pause after each carriage return in the incoming text. In the interim, the computers ignore any incoming characters. Thus it is wise to program in a delay after the transmission of each line. Typically, a one-second wait will satisfy even the most conservative of these mainframes. Thus, in the **Modout** routine (Chapter 7), extra instructions should be inserted to check for a carriage return and pause for a second before going on to the next character to be transmitted.

This type of difficulty is not confined to mainframe computers. Some microcomputer communications systems, such as those that save each incoming line as a separate record on a disk file or those that are temporarily overloaded, may have similar timing problems. If a system still does not respond properly after a one-second delay, try increasing the delay a little. If the system responds readily to the insertion of the delay, try decreasing it until reception problems reappear, then increase the delay by 10% or so to maximize transmission speed. Don't forget that large timesharing systems are likely to have variable response times, depending on their instantaneous load of other communications traffic.

The Periodic Check

DATA BLOCKS. This and the next option require full-duplex operation. Both actively check to see if the computer at the other end is functioning. The least time-consuming means of doing this is to transmit data in blocks. That is, send a group of characters, say 128, out to the other computer, and then wait for the echo of a character, any character, before sending out the next group. Waiting for an echo insures that something is happening at the other end, even though it may not be what is intended. For example, the character coming back from the other end may not be one that was sent to it. It may be a "?" from the other system, indicating confusion or total disbelief about your data stream.

As an example, many minicomputers have a short character buffer (a unit of memory that collects incoming characters until the CPU decides what to do with them). Frequently the buffer is only 80 characters, the length of a Hollerith (IBM) card. If the buffer-equipped computer is busy doing other things while your computer is sending data to it, the buffer may overflow; then the rest of the characters sent to it will simply fall off the end. If you check for an echoed character after one of the 128-byte transmissions you may get one of those that were in the buffer before the fall. Thus there are three types of responses from the other computer in this situation:

1. No character is returned. The system at the other end has given up; or it has sent a character while your system was transmitting but not listening, and your system failed to detect it.

2. A strange character is returned, not one that was sent.

3. A character that may have come from the data group is returned. It may even be the last character sent from your machine.

The first case is clearly an error. Occurrence of this situation tells you that something is wrong. It doesn't tell you what. The second case may or may not indicate an error. If the strange character returned to your system is a "prompt" from the other computer, and the last character sent by your machine was a carriage return, then all may be well. (A prompt is the character or characters that the computer displays at the beginning of each new line when it is ready to receive more instructions, data, text, etc. Examples are: **A:, B:, A>, B>**, etc., for CDOS℠ and CP/M℠ system prompts; @ for DEC TENEX℠ and TOPS℠ executive level prompts; and various other punctuation marks for other systems and/or other program levels within these systems.) If, in the third case, the character returned is the one last sent then the chances are good (but not perfect) that all is well.

RETURN AND PROMPT CHECKING. This system works reasonably well most of the time in typical telephonic data communications. In the simplest case, the transmitting computer simply waits for the echo of a RETURN (0Dh) or a linefeed (0Ah) after each text line it sends. Of course, this requires that the data you are sending include a RETURN every few dozen characters. Since most input buffers on mainframes and minicomputers hold at least one Hollerith cardful of characters (80), the chances are relatively small that overloading problems will plague the systems in this mode of operation. To incorporate this option in the program of Chapter 7, simply add a routine to *Modout* that waits for the echo of a RETURN or a line feed (via *Modin*).

A similar routine in the transmitting computer can sift through incoming characters, echoed or otherwise, until it sees the "go-ahead" prompt from the other machine. The difficulties with this system are two: first, different machines may use different prompt characters to tell you that they are ready to receive data; second, a machine may use different characters at different times, depending on the program mode it is in. If you communicate only with one other type of machine in only one program mode, then all that is necessary is to have the proper prompt character(s) recognized in your software. If you intend to use your computer in communication with a variety of other machines, and you wish to use the appearance of a prompt as the way of confirming that your data were received, then it may be necessary to include a menu of possible prompts to be checked in the communications program. Alternatively, you may wish to be able to enter the appropriate prompt to check, via a console command.

For either of these options it may also be desirable to include a delay prior to starting a new line, for the reasons mentioned earlier. These options are intermediate, in their effects on transmission speed, between the ignorance mode and the thorough, character-by-character checking to be discussed next.

Thorough Error Checking

NONPROTOCOL STYLE. The mode with the greatest potential accuracy is that in which each character transmitted is checked. Each time a character is sent to the other machine, the transmitting machine waits for the character to be echoed. Only after the proper echo is received is the next character transmitted. If the wrong character is echoed then the transmitting machine may simply signal an error or may make an attempt at correcting it. For example, it may send out a DELETE character (FFh), wait for the receipt of a backslash and the erroneous character (or whatever the other computer uses to indicate that it has erased the error), then retransmit the original character. If, after an appropriate interval, no echo at all has been received, then the machine either signals an error or retransmits the character. This is called a "nonprotocol" checking mode because the two machines do not have to follow any fixed, mutually established procedure to accomplish the data transfer or the error checking.

One of the complications of this option is that the receiving machine may send back characters other than those sent to it, such as prompt characters, page header messages, and the like. These are not in any way connected with errors in data transmission but may be interpreted as such by an unsophisticated communication program. People have no trouble coping with these eventualities; computers *do*, if not properly instructed. Prompts are relatively easy to deal with; "header" messages (the messages that appear at the top of the screen for each new screenful in a text-editing program, for example) require much more attention. In practice, the level of complexity required to deal with that level of interaction is beyond the capabilities of any reasonably sized microcomputer communications program (in the early '80s), unless there are only a few headers with which the program must be concerned.

A more basic source of difficulty may be encountered during the error-correction attempt described above. Here the problem is similar to that of prompt-watching: different computers have different modes of error correction. Some demand backspaces to delete characters; some require DELs; some take either; some echo the erroneous character only; some add a backslash or other character to indicate deletion; some just backspace and write the next character over the last one. As in prompt detection, it may be necessary to add more than one routine in the file-transmission module to accommodate the variety of situations.

Finally, the amount of time your machine may be "willing" to wait before retransmitting a "lost" character may depend on what is at the other end. Some busy timesharing machines are notoriously slow during the hours of peak activity. Several seconds may go by, while the machine is servicing other customers, before your last character is echoed. Premature retransmission of the characters by your machine may in these circumstances cause rather than prevent errors.

The reverse problem can also occur. The receiving machine may echo the character before the transmitting machine is ready to accept it back. There may be several reasons for this: the data rate may be so high that the echo returns before a slow microprocessor can go through the program steps between the transmission and the echo watch; the communications software may have too much "overhead," with the same consequences; there may be too many other steps for checking system responses (such as looking for a Control-D from the console) for the data rate being used. In either case the effect is to put an upper limit on the rate at which data can be received. Conversely, if a high data rate is an absolute must then the effect is to limit the complexity of the communications program, or at least to stress the importance of fast, compact code in this portion of the program. The use of 16- or 32-bit microprocessors, separate I/O microprocessors, shorter processor cycle times, or all of these will alleviate this problem in all but the most exotic forms of serial data transmission.

THOROUGH ERROR CHECKING WITH PROTOCOLS.

There is a technique that provides a means for thorough checking of data transmission errors and is relatively fast. Its drawback is that both the sending and the receiving computers must use the same system for data transmission, if not the identical variety of software; that is, it depends on a common communications protocol.

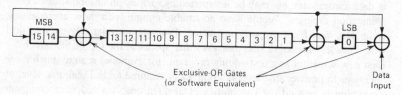

Exclusive-OR Gates
(or Software Equivalent)

Data
Input

Figure 8-1
A Block Check Register (CRC-16)

The simplest way of providing some protection from errors is the parity bit discussed frequently earlier. The rule, when parity is checked, is that all characters transmitted shall have an odd number of ones in them (for odd parity; they have an even number of ones in even parity). Let us examine the transmission of a typical ASCII character, an 'e,' to see what happens. Using one start bit, one stop bit, and odd parity, we construct the transmitted character as follows:

```
ASCII 'e'              1100101

Parity bit              1
                       Stop      Start
Start & Stop bits 1              1

Final character        1111001011
```

Note that the character is sent serially from right to left; the start bit appears at the right end of the character. The parity bit is a *1* in this case because the ASCII 'e' has an even number of *1*s. ASCII 'g' would get a *0* as the parity bit, because it has an odd number of *1*s *(1100111)*. Now, suppose that a noise pulse in the telephone line causes the 'e' to be received as 1111111010, that is, the fifth and sixth bits from the left (bits 4 and 3 in the original data byte) are changed to *1*s. The start and stop bits are stripped off by the receiver, leaving *11111101*. The parity bit is still *1* and the number of *1*s in the remaining ASCII character *(1111101)* is still even so that there is no indication of a parity error. The received character is interpreted as a '}' instead of an 'e'.

In fact, the parity-check method of error detection works only when there are an odd number of bits changed by noise. That will occur more than half the time, because one wrong bit is more likely than two, three more likely than four, and so forth, but "more than half" may not be good enough. For more reliable error detection something more effective is needed.

THE CRC METHOD. The "more effective" system most often used involves the periodic addition of "check characters" to the data stream. In particular, the "cyclic redundancy check" (CRC) method is the one most commonly used for relatively error-free transmission. We will not go into all the details of the CRC method here. There is an extensive literature available that develops the mathematics of the system. However, the principle of operation of the system is a feedback arrangement that uses a set of check registers at the transmitting and receiving ends of the communications link. These registers need not be extra hardware in the microcomputer or the modem; the storage registers of the microprocessor can be used for the purpose.

Figure 8-1 shows the *block check register* that is the heart of the process. It consists of three pieces of register interconnected by "exclusive-OR" gates. Exclusive-Or (or *XOR*) gates transmit *0*s when both inputs are the same, *1*s otherwise. The figure shows the configuration for a standard 16-bit check register, that is, one that works on data in 16-bit chunks. The register is a shift register: the contents of the register get shifted to the right as each new data bit comes in. Let us examine the process in the data transmitter.

First, assume that the register is set to 0 at the beginning of transmission of a block of data. Figure 8-2a shows what happens if a *1* is the first data bit to be transmitted; the *1* appears in all of the components of the register because the inputs to all of the *XOR* gates were *1-0* pairs. Next, suppose that the subsequent bit is a *0*. At the entry *XOR* gate (gate A in the figure) the input is a *0* from the data stream and a *1* from the least-significant-bit cell of the register. Therefore the gate transmits a *1* to the rest of the register. At gate B we have the combination of the *1* from gate A and a *0* from cell 1 of the register. This causes gate B to transmit a *1* to cell 0. At gate C the inputs are the *1* from gate A and the *0* from cell 14 of the register. This causes gate C to transmit a *1* also. Finally, a *1* from gate A goes to cell 15 of the shift register, giving the bit pattern shown in Figure 8-2b.

Next, suppose that a *1* comes from the data stream. Since cell 0 of the register also contains a *1*, gate A transmits a *0*. At gate B a *0* is also transmitted to cell 0 because both inputs to the gate are zeros. Gate C, on the other hand, transmits a *1* because its input from cell 14 is a *1* and that from gate A is a zero. Finally, cell 15 goes to *0* because of the input from gate A.

Clearly, the status of the block check register at any given point in the data transmission process is a complicated function of the details of the data stream. Each new bit has effects that are spread throughout the register.

The data receiver has an identical register that is also set to zero when the data block begins. The only difference is that the incoming, not the transmitted,

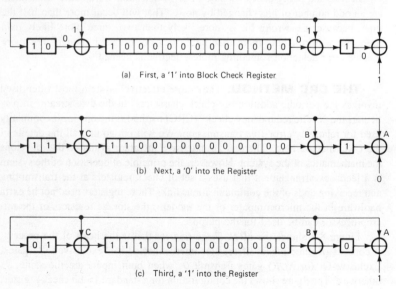

(a)   First, a '1' into Block Check Register

(b)   Next, a '0' into the Register

(c)   Third, a '1' into the Register

Figure 8-2
Data Propagation

data are sent to the register. Now comes the big moment! When all of the data in the block have been sent out by the transmitter, *it then transmits the contents of the shift register* in a 16-bit character (in the example shown) known as the CRC character, least significant bit first. This character is sent to the block check register in the receiver, just as the data bits were.

If the transmission process was noiseless, then the contents of the receiver check register should be identical to those of the transmitter register at the end of the data block. In that case, the first bit of the CRC character should be identical to the bit in cell 0 of the receiver check register, and gate A will send a *0* down the line. When this *0* is applied to the other gates, they will simply shift to the right the contents of the cell to their left. This process will continue until the entire CRC character has been checked. The result is that, because the transmission was noiseless in this example, the register is filled with *0*s.

If there were errors in the transmission, then the chances are very high that the CRC character in the receiver will not match the one sent by the transmitter. Consequently the register will not be zero at the end of the transmission. Any non-zero result is interpreted as a transmission error. The CRC-16 system shown in Figures 8-1 and 8-2 will detect errors due to bursts of noise up to 16 bits in length. It will also detect longer noise bursts more than 99% of the time. At 300 baud a 16-bit error requires continuous noise over a period of about .05 second. This is relatively rare in most telephone traffic in the U.S.

Using CRC: To use the CRC method the transmitting and receiving stations have to have the same check-register setup, and they have to agree on the length of the data block to be transmitted, as well as all the other details on character length, etc. Once this is done, the procedure is quite simple. First, the transmitting station sends a standard-length data block, say 256 bytes, while running the data through its check register. The transmitter appends the two-byte CRC character to the end of the data block (assuming the system just described is used) and waits.

The receiver also sends the incoming data stream through its check register, while keeping track of the number of bytes received. At 258 bytes (256 plus the CRC character), the contents of the check register are examined. If the register is filled with *0*s the receiver sends the transmitter a prearranged signal to send the next block. If the register indicates an error, the receiver sends a signal (typically a NAK or Control-U) to retransmit the block. It then flushes the data block just received and waits for the retransmission.

This process has some fringe benefits. First, it eliminates the requirement that the receiver have a very large memory by making it possible to save each successfully received data block on disk before sending the go-ahead signal to the transmitter. Second, the transmission/reception process is relatively simple, because of the strict protocol involved, so that there is no worry about such things as ambiguous prompts and extra characters. Third, it can be tailored to the communicating systems to make the best use of their capabilities, by adjusting the size of the data blocks, the size of the check register, and the transmission rate. Fourth, the technique is very useful for transmitting binary files, as opposed to ASCII characters, where there are no (or at least fewer) worries about various control characters and other non-ASCII data doing strange things to the program; the program is constructed simply to ignore the meaning of any incoming bytes. Finally, the "overhead" of the system is relatively low, consisting of only two bytes per data block, so the transmission speed and accuracy can be made simultaneously high.

THE BINARY SYNCHRONOUS (BISYNC) PROTOCOL.

One particular version of this technique, pioneered by IBM for communications between its mainframes and peripherals such as card readers and punches used as remote batch terminals, is called BISYNC. The logical reasons for this are that it concerns itself with binary data (which may also be ASCII or EBCDIC characters), and it is a byte-synchronous protocol. That is, unlike all of the asynchronous communications methods we have discussed thus far, BISYNC uses a central clock to synchronize the fixed-rate transmission between the communicating components. BISYNC was first used by IBM in 1965 and has since become an industry-standard method of data transmission.

BISYNC uses a form of the block-transmission CRC-error-checking routine just described. It is a half-duplex protocol; only one terminal can send data on the line at a time. If no terminal is transmitting in a BISYNC system, that is, if the terminals are "idling," then a terminal desiring to send a message must first send a "line bid" signal (an ENQ or Control-B) to the controlling computer. When the line bid has been acknowledged (by an ACK or Control-F), the terminal may send a block of data. Each data block is composed of four main parts: an STX (Start of Text) character; the text of binary data; an ETX or ETB character; and a CRC character. The text portion of the block can be variable in length in some cases.

Two types of data may be sent with BISYNC: character (or nontransparent) and "transparent" data. This is possible because the software in the receiver can be set not to analyze incoming data for content. Thus, data resembling control signals are ignored by the system in the transparent mode. The transparent data field is preceded by the pair "DLE STX" and ended by the pair "DLE ETX" (or "DLE ETB"). A problem would occur in this system if the data being transmitted ever included any of the three pairs of bytes above, which would activate the "switches" in the receiver software. This problem is avoided by "doubling" the marker character if it is *not* to be read as part of a switch-activating pair. In this protocol, a DLE occurring as data would be sent as DLE DLE, and the software switches would be set to respond only to an STX, ETX, or ETB following a solitary DLE. In the transparent mode the data are transmitted as a series of fixed-length records; any unfilled records are padded to the fixed length with zeros or blanks. This causes a disadvantage in the speed of transmission, compared with that of the nontransparent mode. The compensating advantage is of course that *any* data can be transmitted by means of the transparent mode.

In the nontransparent or character mode the records transmitted can be of variable length. However, certain characters are prohibited from being included in the nontransparent data files, so as not to confuse the system. These are: SOH, STX, ETX, EOT, ENQ, DLE, NAK, SYN, ETB, GS, RS, and US (see Table 6-2). Thus a typical nontransparent data block transmission would look like this:

```
STX VDATA RS VDATA RS ... VDATA RS ETB CRC
```

where VDATA is a variable length data block. A transparent data transmission (for IBM 2770, 2968, 3741 terminals) would look like this:

```
DLE STX FDATA FDATA FDATA FDATA ... FDATA DLE ETB CRC
```

In this case FDATA is a fixed-length data block. As is intimated above, the details of the protocol differ slightly, depending on which IBM terminal one is emulating.

BISYNC is ordinarily used at high baud rates, from 1200 to 9600 baud, over ordinary telephone lines. Because of the higher costs of modems in this range BISYNC is not ordinarily used for occasional or casual computer communications.

OTHER THOUGHTS ON DATA TRANSFER

Binary file transfer is effectively carried out using a protocol error checking system such as that just described. This is probably the best way to transmit such files. Another technique is to convert the data in the files into strings of hexadecimal numbers represented alphanumerically. This is required if one of the computers in the exchange can handle only 7-bit characters, as is often the case. Upon receipt, these alphanumeric strings can be reconverted to binary and handled appropriately. The technique for doing this in BASIC is relatively simple, as demonstrated here:

```
10    Rem Binary-to-Hex/ASCII Converter
20    Dim Block$(127) : Index=0 : Endfile=0 : Rem A 128 byte block size
30    Open\1,128\Filename$ : Rem First open the binary file
40    On Error Goto Finisher : Rem Error occurs at End of File

50  #Starter : While Endfile=0 : Rem read the data until the end is reached
60      Get\1,Index\Block$
70        For I=0 To 63 : Rem Take two bytes at a time
80          Character1=Asc(Block$(2*I,2*I)) : Rem Convert them to ASCII
90          Character2=Asc(Block$(2*I+1,2*I+1))
100         Character$=Hex$(Character1+Character2*128) : Rem and to hex
110         Print Character$;" "; : Rem ... and send them out
120       Next I
130     Index=Index+1
140   Endwhile
150   Print "The End";Chr$(7)

170 #Finisher : Close : Endfile=-1 : Goto Starter
```

This method is still somewhat convoluted because of BASIC's reluctance to deal directly with hexadecimal numbers when conversing with the programmer. First, the binary file must be invoked as if it were a character file. This may require a temporary change of the file name for some dialects of BASIC. Next the individual bytes are selected, and converted into representative ASCII values from 0 to 255. Note from this that it is possible to have ASCII values greater than 127, even though most transmissions of text do not use the eighth bit. Finally, the ASCII value of the byte is translated into a hexadecimal representation for final transmission. In the dialect used in the example, the hex values are always presented in groups of four characters. Hence the original bytes are taken two at a time to satisfy this quirk.

This technique, or a variation of it, is also useful to include in the program when there may be interface problems in the system. If one computer may be sending the other control characters that are causing strange responses, then it may be wise to convert all incoming bytes into hexadecimal numbers before they get to the affected computer's operating system. This way they are both rendered harmless and are made visible to the console so that the offenders can be located—at the expense of "throughput" speed.

AUTOMATIC LOGIN

Another enhancement for decreasing the dreariness of the login routine, and incidentally making it easier to use for inexperienced operators, is to make it all automatic. Since we have conjured a routine for automatically dialing another computer, it is but a small step to have automatic login. Although small, this step is not trivial. Take the example given in Figure 4-1. It begins after the dialing process is completed and the connection between the computers has been established. The other machine first appears, in the example, by sending an @ as a prompt.

The automatic logger-in would see this as the opportunity to transmit its standard message, contained in a program line somewhere, "log jdoe zbgrg5 12345". The transmitting program may then wait patiently for the next @ to appear, whereupon it may send its master a message to go ahead. That is all there is to it in a simple situation such as the one described. Other login protocols may be more complicated, requiring other exchanges between the transmitting and the receiving computer but this general routine holds for all of them. Its primary drawback is that it requires extra memory space if it is to be a permanent part of the program; it may be considered a poor use of the space if memory is tight.

USE WITH OTHER MODEMS

All of the material in the examples above is for a particular language-modem combination: Cromemco 32K Structured BASIC and the D. C. Hayes Micromodem 100. Very little change in concept is required for other languages or for other types of modems. In many cases only the details of the control words and/ or the locations of the data and control ports have to be changed. In others where

Figure 8-3
D.C. Hayes Smartmodem
(Courtesy of Hayes Microcomputer Products, Inc.)

some capabilities are not available, or where capabilities more extensive than those of the D. C. Hayes modem are possible, more extensive program changes may be desired.

For example, the Potomac Micro (PMMI) modem has two control ports, a baud rate port, and a data port—in contrast to the D. C. Hayes Micromodem's data, status/control, second control, and timer ports. Control bytes are all different. The chief effect of all of these variations is to give sleepless nights to the hardy programmers who produce "universal" software for data communications. If you intend to write your own programs for data transmission, and write them for a single type of modem, the task is much simpler; adapt the procedures discussed earlier to the details of the system you will be using.

In some cases the programmable modem need not be a physical part of the microcomputer system. For example, the D. C. Hayes "Smartmodem" (Figure 8-3) is fully programmable by means of a simple series of one- or two-character commands sent to it via a standard serial interface from the host computer. In this version, a ROM within the modem package itself has the facility for translating these commands into the appropriate modem actions. The Smartmodem also includes a small loudspeaker so that the caller can hear the traffic over the phone line. This is rather boring in most circumstances but can be quite useful when you are trying to discover why the initial connection with the other computer has not taken place. (Is the machine not answering, is the line busy, did you get a person instead?)

There were a few dozen types of relatively low-cost modems available in the early 1980s (modems with prices under $300). All of them had maximum transmission rates of 300 (or possibly 600) baud. In 1982, several modems for microcomputers with 300 and 1200 baud capability were introduced, costing less than $600. All of them are amenable to the types of control outlined in these chapters. As the pace of microelectronics development increases, and as the effects of increased competition in the telecommunications industry become more widespread, the microcomputer owner will find a growing array of possibilities for telecommunications opening up. In the remaining chapters, some of these possibilities will be discussed.

9

Most intercomputer telecommunication connections involve the use of some sort of telecommunication network. The most common example of this is the switched telephone system. All of the preceding chapters have gone on the assumption that the user will be dealing with such a system at least part of the time. Certainly, the telephone system will be the telecommunications medium for many of the applications to be discussed in the concluding chapter.

The telephone system is, however, by no means the only telecommunication medium open to microcomputers. A growing number of microcomputers will be interacting over other kinds of telecommunication networks. The three most likely carriers for these other forms of computer communication are CATV systems, radio, and "local networks." Each of these modes has its own set of hardware and software/protocol requirements. This chapter reviews some of the issues in each of these areas.

SOME DESIGN CHOICES

No communication network, human or artificial, is without limitations of some sort. The ideal system might be one in which the human and machine participants communicate with each other telepathically; that is to say, directly with each other's "brains." Unfortunately (maybe), we have not yet reached that stage of evolution. Meanwhile, the designers of practical telecommunication networks have to make compromises among a number of factors such as:

● **Flexibility**—How alterable are the communications paths?

● **Connectivity**—To how many others can a communicator talk? Just one, all other users, or only some others? Can many different communicator-pair conversations occur simultaneously over the network?

● **Scope**—How many people (or machines) are connected or connectable to the network?

● **Accuracy/fidelity**—How imperfect is the delivered communication when compared with what the sender was thinking at the time?

● **Bandwidth/richness**—How many subtleties of the communication process does the medium deliver? What is the variety of communication modes available to the user?

Concepts of
Telecommunication Networks

- **Simultaneity**—Is the communication instantaneous or are delays involved?

- **Reliability**—Is the network always available to all the users or is some number of failures allowable?

- **Cost**—What must the user pay, in both initial and operating expenses, to use the system?

The first three of these factors, flexibility, connectivity and scope, are characteristics of the *topology* of a network. They determine physical access to the network and the ways in which users of the network may interact. The next four factors affect the variety and utility of the communications that can be carried on over the network. The final factor, of course, determines the economic accessibility of the network. It is affected by all of the other factors and by the underlying technology. The relative importances of these factors determine the practical realization of the network.

As an example, let us examine the U.S. telephone system using these factors. Great emphasis has been placed on flexibility. It should be possible to communicate with anyone connected to the network over a variety of different paths. Connectivity is also a prime consideration; anyone connected to the network can communicate with anyone else and even with groups of others. Since the network employs separate lines to individual subscribers, the number of separate conversations that can be carried on over the network is limited only by the number of switches available in the intervening switching centers. Bidirectionality is important here; unlike unidirectional broadcast systems, the telephone system allows two-way and even multi-way communications. Scope is also very important; most U.S. households have telephones (although apparently not quite as many as have TV sets). In short, the telephone system is a large, highly connective, flexible network.

Accuracy or fidelity is not of overwhelming significance in the telephone system, as we have seen. The system depends on the ability of the human brain-ear combination to identify the speaker at the other end of the line and to sort the essence of the conversation out of the background noise and the restricted spectrum. The high redundancy of human speech greatly helps this task. Computers, with no such brain capacity, and often with considerably less redundant messages to transmit, have problems with this tradeoff, as we have seen.

The bandwidth of the telephone system is limited to the portion of the audio spectrum that encompasses most of the distinguishing characteristics of human speech. As it turns out, this is sufficient to convey a considerable range of subtleties of expression to humans communicating with each other. Far richer telecommunication modes, such as TV, use considerably more bandwidth (by a factor of more than 1000) without transmitting much more basic information. The extra bandwidth is used for rapidly transmitting a large amount of redundant information expressing small increments to the basic data. That is, moving pictures are even more redundant than human speech. The first picture may be worth 1000 words, but the next several depicting almost the same scene are worth very little more. Add bidirectionality to this process and the costs double because analog picture information cannot be transmitted simultaneously in both directions over a telecommunication channel.

Computer communication systems have the same dilemma. The telephone system serves as an adequate medium for relatively low-speed transmission of text material. It is unsuitable, in its present state, for rapid transmission of large amounts of computer graphic materials, such as might be desired for real-time moving-graphics communications (interactive, three-dimensional galactic exploration games, for example).

Simultaneity has been another main selling point of the telephone system. There is as much simultaneity in a telephone conversation as in a face-to-face conversation, except for the quarter-second path delay in trans-global conversations via communications satellite. Microcomputer telecommunications via the telephone or any other telecommunications system have similar simultaneity considerations. In one sense, microcomputer communications can be "more simultaneous." With electronic mail, the two conversants can hold a discussion even if they are never connected to the system at the same time—a feat not possible with ordinary telephone conversations. On the other hand, two microcomputer operators typing at each other via the telephone system are engaging in a much less efficient information transfer process than if they were talking to each other using a common vocal language.

Reliability also gets a high ranking in the design criteria of the telephone system. Although we tend to complain mightily about poor telephone service, few human-produced systems are more reliable. In fact, many of our contemporary means of assessing reliability derive from research carried out at AT&T's Bell Labs.

Finally, the provision of all these capabilities at moderate cost is a major factor in the design of the telephone system. Clearly, government regulation has been a major influence in this regard but, with the separation of the local operating companies from AT&T and increased competition in the data communications field, we can expect to see low telecommunications costs (relative to other service costs) continue.

In summary, the telephone system represents a well-considered selection of design factors oriented toward giving the largest number of human users efficient, effective, two-way telecommunications at a relatively low cost. No wonder, then, that it is likely to be the medium of choice for a large number of communications between microcomputers.

There is another factor, not explicitly mentioned above because, in the past, it generally has not been a major factor in the design of a communications network. This is the factor of the generality and utility of communications protocols used on the network. For the telephone system the primary protocol is that of establishing the connection between two or more parties; the human participants take care of the protocols after that. In a switched or private-line telephone system the protocol issues are not very much more complicated even for computer telecommunications. Some relatively simple rules can be established that, if followed by all participants, make communications straightforward and easy. For some other forms of telecommunications networks the protocol problems are more complex. The following sections treat some of these problems. One fundamental protocol problem in data transmission is that of identifying data as originating from a specific source when several sources may be transmitting on a single communications path. This problem hinders achieving the goal of maintaining high connectivity while minimizing the use of scarce resources.

MAINTAINING CONNECTIVITY— SWITCHING METHODS

There are several ways of maintaining high connectivity over a communications network. In the telephone system the dominant technique is switching of twisted-pair telephone lines. Each conversation or data transmission uses a unique pair of wires connecting the conversants. This requires a substantial investment just in wires connecting the various subscribers to the system; there are more than one billion miles of telephone wire in the United States. Most of those wires are unused most of the time, because they are not carrying messages. Suppose that we are interested in building a communications network among computers that does not have to rely on separate pairs of wires for all the participants. In this case more efficient sharing of some of the capital resources, such as interconnecting cables, becomes an important advantage. The question is, how can it be done?

Multiplexing

One of the techniques for stuffing different communications into the same physical transmission facilities is called multiplexing. There are two basic modes of multiplexing, using the two main domains in which signals exist: time and frequency. Figure 9-1a presents the basic concept of multiplexing: a number of individual incoming signals are transformed by the multiplexor into a single stream of signals which are then transmitted over a single transmission line. At the other end of the line a demultiplexor, like a modem, transforms the transmission back into a series of separate signals.

In "Time-Division Multiplexing" (TDM), Figure 9-1b, the incoming messages, A, B and C in the figure, are each split into a series of short segments. The segments from the different message sources are then precisely interleaved, each segment in its own time slot, and sent over the transmission line as if they were a single signal. That is, they take only the frequency space, the bandwidth, of a single signal. This version of multiplexing is therefore useful for systems that are confined to the use of limited-bandwidth transmissions lines, such as long twisted-pair cables. Its drawback is that the multiplexing process produces delays in transmission; the last part of each message arrives later than it would if there were no other messages being transmitted. Further, the added delay is proportional to the number of different signals that the system is designed to transmit. because each signal is assigned its own time slot.

TDM systems also have some system-induced error problems. First, it is important to make sure that the incoming data segments are identified correctly by the demultiplexor. This is usually accomplished by coding some sort of identification into each data element transmitted. This code may indicate only the start of the data element, that is the beginning (or end, or both) of the data frame, or it may explicitly identify the signal source. This feature also generally solves the second system error problem: timing. TDM systems are usually synchronous. Unlike the asynchronous transmission methods we have been discussing primarily thus far, in which signals could be sent and received at random times, TDM requires precise timing to ensure that the messages do not get garbled.

A variant of TDM uses a separate address block for each segment of data transmitted. This enables the blocks to be addressed dynamically, in response to the incoming signal traffic. This technique is variously called "Statistical Time-Division Multiplexing" (STDM), "Dynamically Addressed Multiplexing" (DAM), or "Concentration." As illustrated in Figure 9-1c, the signal segments are not strictly interleaved in this method. Rather, they are sent out on what amounts to a first-come, first-served basis. The separate address blocks take care of the timing and identification problems and the dynamic addressing acts to reduce the delays inherent in the simpler TDM systems. Statistical multiplexing is becoming an increasingly popular means of linking small local groups of computers or computer peripherals to external communications networks.

In "Frequency-Division Multiplexing" (FDM), as shown in Figure 9-1d, the available signals are transmitted simultaneously, but at different frequencies. The situation is similar to conventional radio or TV broadcasts: each originating signal goes out over its own channel. For additional safety from interchannel interference each channel is usually separated from its neighbors by a narrow *guard band*. The advantage of FDM is that simultaneity is preserved; no additional delays are imposed by the transmission process. The disadvantage is that the transmission cable is more complex and expensive than a twisted pair if a

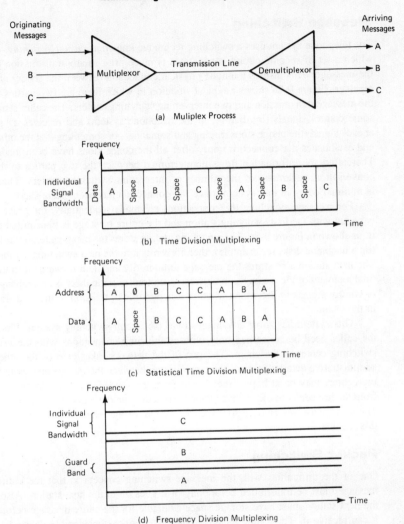

(a) Muliplex Process

(b) Time Division Multiplexing

(c) Statistical Time Division Multiplexing

(d) Frequency Division Multiplexing

Figure 9-1
Multiplexing Concepts

large number of signals are to be carried simultaneously over a considerable distance (more than fifty feet or so). FDM is commonly used in the long-distance leg of telephone transmissions, where hundreds of simultaneous conversations are carried over wideband cables or satellite links. It is also the method used for CATV transmission and associated data services, as they become available.

Message Switching

The telephone system uses a switching technique known as *circuit switching*, in which a set of specific circuit connections is made prior to any transmission of the message. This insures a unique physical connection between the sender and receiver. Figure 9-2a shows a typical situation in which there are two parties to the message transmission and two intervening switching centers. The caller sends some control signals (by dialing, in the telephone system) and receives a "go ahead" signal (the phone stops ringing and someone—or something—at the other end establishes the connection) only after all the connections have been made. Thereafter, the information flows uninterrupted between the two parties to the conversation, regardless of the number of intervening switching centers. There is minimal delay in this system, once the connection has been established.

For message switching the connections are made sequentially; the process is begun with the first switching station and the entire message is transmitted to it, as shown in Figure 9-2c. The switching station stores the message temporarily (on a magnetic disk, for example), then forwards it to the next switching station. The next station also stores the message temporarily and then forwards it to the final recipient of the message. In between each transmission there is an exchange of control signals to determine whether it is possible to transmit to the next link in the chain.

This system has some advantages over the circuit-switching system. First, the caller need be concerned only with establishing connections with the first switching center in the chain. The rest of the network takes care of the other administrative details. Second, the transmission between the intervening switching centers may be at higher speed than from the sender to the first center, or from the last center to the receiver, thereby speeding up the transmission process. The Telex networks and the AUTODIN I system of the federal government use this method.

Packet Switching

One of the difficulties with the message-switching concept is that the entire message must be transmitted before any of it goes on to the next station. Also, the next station must have storage space available for the entire message before it can receive it. Thus, long messages may experience considerable delays between transmission from the originator and receipt by the intended recipient. A technique that overcomes these difficulties, while retaining the possibility for high-speed transmission between the intervening switching centers, is called packet switching.

Figure 9-2d shows the concept. The message is broken up into small, uniform-sized increments—"packets." When the end of the first packet is received by the first switching center it immediately starts the process of retransmission to the next center. The next center also begins retransmission immediately after it receives the end of the first packet from the first center, and so on. In the

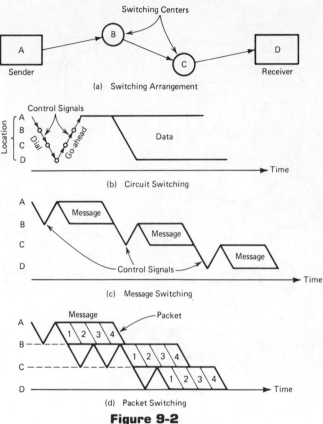

Figure 9-2
Switching Techniques

figure some extra delays have been put in to indicate that switching centers B and C are briefly busy. In ordinary (low-to-moderate) traffic circumstances there would be no such additional delays and the first packet would reach the receiver very shortly after its transmission by the sender.

Even the small delays added in the later stage of the process shown in Figure 9-2d can be avoided in a sophisticated packet-switching system. For example, there may be another switching center, E, located elsewhere that can transmit to D and is not busy at the time. The packets would then be routed via E instead of C. With this "dynamic-switching" method the network controllers can always act to route the packets to the destination with minimal delay. In fact, during heavy system traffic, the various component packets of the message may travel widely different physical routes before they are finally assembled at the receiver's site.

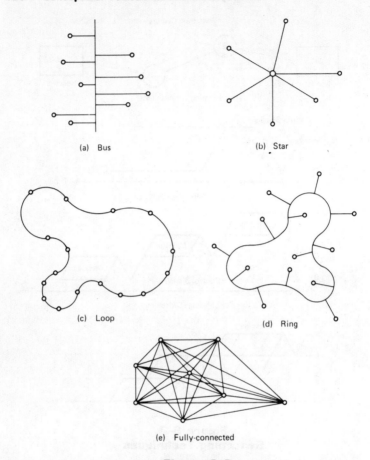

(a) Bus

(b) Star

(c) Loop

(d) Ring

(e) Fully-connected

Figure 9-3
Network Topologies

Because of the speed and flexibility of packet switching, many commercial data transmission networks are now using the concept. These include GTE's TELENET, the TYMNET system and the Satellite Business System networks. Most new commercial data transmission networks will probably use some form of packet switching as their primary mode of transmission—even for voice signals. The latter development still awaits some perfection in the laboratories before it becomes widely available but it is inevitable.

Like STDM both message switching and packet switching require that the messages or the packets have some identifying data attached to them. The specific modes for attaching the required identifiers, the methods for minimizing transmission errors, and the development of standards for all of these are the subject of a large and continuing effort by organizations in the international telecommunication community. Since most of these issues deal with the long-haul task of transmission between the switching centers, rather than with the local task of transmission between a microcomputer and a switching center, they are not treated here. However, the reader may wish to get a better understanding of the complexities of these issues through reading some of the references in the bibliography. In practice, it may not be necessary to become acquainted with all of the gory details. Semiconductor manufacturers will already have the international protocols for packet switching (CCITT Recommendation X.25) incorporated into single chips. For example, the Western Digital WD2501 packet-network interface, a 48-pin chip, performs this key role for a microcomputer that is to be directly involved in packet switching.

Thus far we have been referring frequently to these shadowy networks that seem to hold the key to long-distance communication among microcomputers. It is time to see what sort of creatures these networks are.

TYPES OF NETWORKS

Networks can be characterized by their "topology," the pattern of interconnection of their elements. There are five basic network topologies, three of which were shown in Figure 3-1. Figure 9-3 repeats those three and adds the other two. These different patterns are known as the bus, the star, the loop, the ring, and the fully connected topology.

The fully connected topology, as you recall, was characteristic of the telephone and telegraph systems in their early stages of development. There is a direct, "dedicated" connection between each pair of communicators.

The bus topology is characteristic of the party line and of the internal architecture of the microprocessor and the microcomputer. Each potential communicator has access to the common communication path. The individual communicators can be of widely varying capabilities.

The star topology characterizes the simple contemporary telephone exchange. The central node in the star is responsible for switching all of the messages between communicators. The central node must be capable of all the switching and communications functions of the network, so the outlying nodes need not be very intelligent or capable. The typical computer time-sharing system also is a star network; in this case the central node (the main computer) is also the terminus of most of the communications traffic. This is the preferred topology when low-cost, flexible-path, randon-time-of-arrival communication is desired, as is the case for the two examples given. If the central node "crashes," that is, goes out of commission, so does the communications system, but if the mainframe in a time-sharing system crashes, of what use is the system anyway?

The loop topology is often used to interconnect a series of similar machines, such as microcomputers. In this topology each node is responsible for passing on messages sent to it by an adjoining node, unless, of course, it is the message recipient. Each node in the loop must be capable of all the communications functions of the network. If any node in the loop crashes, so does the system. The old parlor game of "Pass it on" uses a loop network with, it is hoped, hilarious results because of message retransmission errors.

Finally, the ring network is sort of a combination of the bus and loop topologies. The ring itself acts like a conveyor belt; message "bins" continually circulate around the ring in a single direction. Nodes put messages into a passing empty bin or take out messages addressed to them as they come by. The "bin" is a permission code or "token" generated by the loop controller. If an individual node on the ring crashes, there is no effect on the ring operation since, unlike the loop topology, the node is not directly in the communications path.

Note that it is not necessary that there be a physical, permanent connection between all the nodes of these topologies. There are many instances of wireless connections between nodes in a network. For example, the mobile telephone service is a dual-level star network, with one star connected via radio to mobile units. The central node of that star is connected to one or more other twisted-pair telephone distribution systems.

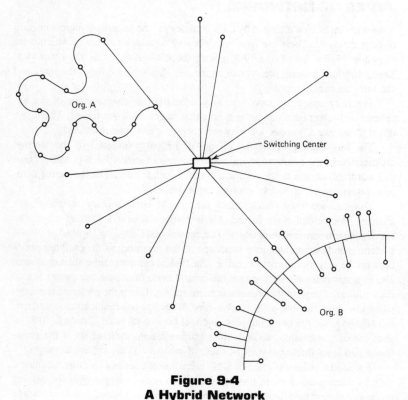

Figure 9-4
A Hybrid Network

Further, all sorts of hybrid topologies are possible, using one topology for one part of the network, others for other parts. For example, Figure 9-4 depicts two specialized networks, each with its own topology, connected to a star network. Let us call the loop network Organization L and the bus network Organization B. Organization L and Organization B might be expected to have their own, different sets of requirements for communication among their members. They also have the need for occasional communication with others outside, via the star network. Both of these local networks might have a number of computers and related peripheral devices that frequently are required to communicate with each other. They are *local* networks because they are designed to cope with the specific communications problems of a single organization, such as a school, a company, a laboratory, or a government agency. The outside star system could be the conventional telephone system, useful because it is optimized to meet the general communication requirements of the larger outside community. The local network, on the other hand, must be responsive to the particular requirements of the organization using it. If these requirements are different from those used to develop the telephone system then we can expect that the resulting network will also differ.

NETWORK CONTROL

As you probably inferred from their descriptions, different network topologies have different control problems. A star network requires that there be a central switching system that is able to handle all of the incoming calls in a reasonable length of time, at least under most conditions. If there are many subscribers to the network who communicate frequently with each other for extended periods of time, then the center has to have many pairs of switches to handle the load. If subscribers communicate with each other infrequently, and only for short periods when they do, then just a few switches will handle the job. Telephone switching centers are "sized" by these considerations.

Multiply connected systems have essentially no control problems since all the subscribers have direct lines to those with whom they wish to communicate. Their problem is more likely to be financial and environmental: how to pay for all those interconnections and what to do with all those wires.

Loop networks also have relatively few control problems; each message from one subscriber to another simply passes through all the intervening subscribers on the way. The problems with loop networks tend to center on error prevention (because of the multiple receptions and relays of the messages), reduced simultaneity (from the same source), and vulnerability to a defunct node. If the loop is physically small, such as a classroom with 25 microcomputers connected together, then these problems are generally not significant. They are likely to be outweighed by the relatively low cost of the network hardware.

The last two communication topologies, the bus and the ring, do have control problems because they are both essentially party-line systems. The basis of the control problem is "contention." Contention occurs when two or more subscribers try to communicate simultaneously and hence interfere with each other. Communication protocols play an important part in sorting out contending traffic. Of course, one approach in the design of a telecommunications system would be not to use a bus or ring structure at all, and thereby eliminate all these difficulties at the outset. Unfortunately, for many types of communications situations, such as two-way cable TV (a double ring system) or many forms of radio telecommunications (a bus structure with the "ether" acting as the bus), there are compelling reasons to use these topologies.

Contention-Resolution Protocols

In a human telephone conversation on a party line (ring topology), the protocol goes something like: "Harry Parsons, get off the line! This has nothing to do with you!" This may not stop Harry from listening, but it should reduce the number of his interruptions. Actually, computer contention protocols are not much different in concept from that one-way conversation. In polite society, the party wishing to communicate listens first to see if anyone else is talking. If no one is, then the caller sends a message down the line with the callee's address (phone number) and waits for a response. If the callee answers, the conversation continues until it is completed, whereupon both parties get off the line. If the line normally carries heavy traffic then the various subscribers agree among themselves that their conversations shall be limited to a given duration.

Another way of handling the problem is to set up the party line so that an individual caller cannot make a call without permission, usually in the form of some sort of signal from the line controller. This is much like the situation in a classroom, a congressional debate, or a committee meeting. Each would-be communicator raises a hand when the previous speaker has finished. Only the one who receives the nod gets to speak next. The following are some examples of systems using contention protocols.

ALOHANET. The ALOHANET was the first major development of a telecommunications system using contention protocols. As its name suggests, ALOHANET was developed in Hawaii, as a means of linking a central computer with terminals scattered among the islands. Each terminal has a radio transceiver (transmitter-receiver), a small local processor, and a small "buffer storage" (that is, a small RAM memory holding a few dozen or a few hundred characters). A terminal intending to communicate with the central computer forms a short message containing an address, the block of accumulated characters, and a count of the characters (a "checksum"), which it transmits to the computer. If there is no contention for the computer's time, an acknowledgment is sent to the terminal. If there was a conflicting message from another terminal, then no acknowledgment is sent. In the latter case, the terminal waits some random length of time and retransmits the message. As is the case with all contention systems, the likelihood that a message will have to be retransmitted increases with the communications traffic. In the case of ALOHANET the contention problem exists only for traffic from the remote terminals to the central computer, because the computer is the only transmitter in the return direction.

SATNET. SATNET was developed by the Advanced Research Projects Agency of the U.S. Department of Defense, developers of the packet-switching concept and of the first large-scale packet-switching network, ARPANET. It is composed of a communications satellite and a number of contending ground stations in a mode similar to that of ALOHANET. Because the satellite is only a relay rather than the central station, however, there are contention possibilities in both directions. Further, the data streams are at much higher rates (megabits per second) than those of ALOHANET, exacerbating the contention problem. The primary means of alleviating contention is to convert from random transmission times to a synchronized transmission system. All of the ground stations are synchronized to a single clock. Each station's data packets (it is a packet transmission system) must be sent only during specific time slots, as in a TDM system. This measure reduces the contention problem by a factor of two, at a small cost in speed of transmission.

ETHERNET

ETHERNET is a local network system developed jointly by Xerox, Intel, and Digital Equipment Corporation, and based on an experimental system in use for several years at Xerox's Palo Alto Research Center. Many microcomputers of the future will be interconnected by some form of local network, so it is worth going into some detail here about the main characteristics of ETHERNET and other forms of local networking.

The basic concept of a local network is, as the name implies, one of economically tying together a number of computing elements that are located in fairly close physical proximity. The idea is that a local network can achieve goals for network communications different from those achieved by the telephone system or other large-scale networks. Particularly important is that local networks allow convenient sharing of scarce or expensive computing facilities such as printers, plotters, high-speed modems or concentrators, mainframe computers, specialized terminals, large data bases, and so on, within a single organization. As a consequence, local networks are one of the favorite topics of those engaged in development of the so-called "office of the future." ETHERNET is prominent among the possible candidates for this all-purpose local telecommunications carrier because of the extensive amount of development and testing that has already been carried out on it, not to mention the fact that it is being advanced by major firms in the industry.

The basic concept of ETHERNET is shown in Figure 9-5. The main element of the network is a "passive" coaxial cable—one which does not have its own active controller to establish timing and resolve contention. The cable is capped by a pair of terminators to prevent signal reflections. The "stations" that are

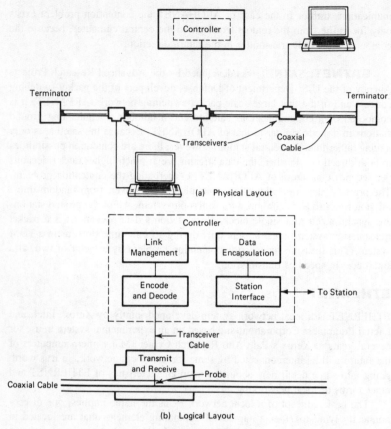

(a) Physical Layout

(b) Logical Layout

Figure 9-5
ETHERNET Concept

connected to the cable can be "workstations" (dumb or intelligent terminals) or any computing facility, such as the ones mentioned above as being scarce or expensive. The stations are connected to the cable via a transceiver-connector, a transceiver cable, and a controller. The controller is likely to be on a circuit board that plugs directly into the innards of the station, although it may also be an external box that communicates with the station via something like an RS-232 interface (for example).

To visualize how this could work in practice, imagine a building containing a number of microcomputers, a few printers, some dumb terminals, an optical character reader, and a high-speed plotter. A coaxial cable is snaked through the walls, or the air conditioning ducts, or the false ceilings of the rooms, so that the cable is within ten or fifteen feet or so of every one of these computing

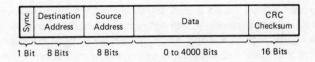

Sync	Destination Address	Source Address	Data	CRC Checksum
1 Bit	8 Bits	8 Bits	0 to 4000 Bits	16 Bits

Figure 9-6
ETHERNET Packet Structure

stations. Each station is then equipped with a controller, an interface cable, and a connector that fits around the cable. Inside the connector is a small, pointed probe that (ideally) punctures the side of the cable, touches the center conductor and makes the physical connection between the station and the cable. Of course, this connector has to be very carefully designed so that it does not cause interference with (or loss of) the signal traffic on the cable. That is all there is to it, except for a few software problems. In principle, all of the stations on the cable can now talk to each other. The software problems arise from the attempt to convert this promise into reality.

Individual ETHERNET cables can be interconnected by the simple expedient of having one of the stations close to both cables act as a repeater. This station is connected to both cables; it is the only station that is connected to both, although each cable can be connected to more than one other cable (each connection-pair via a unique repeater). Each message appearing on cable A is repeated and fed into cable B and vice versa. Thus there is room for expandability of an ETHERNET installation.

The communications traffic problems of ETHERNET are the same as those of the ALOHANET system, except that each station can act as both a transmitter and reciver of data. The general process of signaling is similar, however, A station wishing to send a message to another station prepares a packet containing the data, a source identifier, a destination identifier and a CRC checksum (see Chapter 8). This task is performed by the data encapsulation component of the controller (Figure 9-5b). A single packet is structured as is shown in Figure 9-6.

The link-management part of the controller deals with the message contention issues and, in systems that also have frequency division multiplexing, with channel allocation. ETHERNET does not use FDM; rather, it is a "baseband" system: the signal is sent to the cable without modulating a carrier signal. (There are contending versions of local networks that use "broadband" protocols with FDM.) The encode and decode portion of the controller takes care of synchronization and of encoding and decoding between binary data and the phase modulation used for the signal that is actually transmitted down the cable. Finally, the transceiver does the actual transmission or reception of the signal, senses whether there is already traffic on the channel, and indicates cases of contention to the link-management portion of the controller.

This nice, logical process has been given the imposing title of Carrier-Sense Multiple Access with Collision Detection, or CSMA-CD. Once you know what all that means it seems simple indeed, and the name fits nicely. The transceiver looks for a carrier from another station before transmitting. If there is one already present it notifies the link manager which, in turn, waits for a random period of time before telling the transmitter to try again, and so on. Further, if the transceiver detects interference after it has already started transmission it aborts the transmission and initiates the random wait process. In ETHERNET the mean period before retransmission is adjusted by recent collision history to optimize the probability of error-free transmission. Transmission rates on ETHERNET range from one to ten megabits per second (0.125 to 1.25 million bytes per second). Some of the broadband local-network schemes, such as that of Wang Laboratories, Inc., have transmission rates up to 50 million bits per second. These rates are likely to increase as the technology improves.

Transmission on ETHERNET is essentially immediate if there are no other stations on line or where the number of stations is small. As the number of stations using the network rises, so too does the number of contentions and the signal delays. The severity of delays introduced by contention varies primarily as a function of the length of the packets; the longer the packet (up to the allowable maximum of 1500 bytes) the more efficient the channel use. The recommended maximum number of nodes on an ETHERNET segment is 1024. Tests of the ETHERNET system at the Palo Alto Research Center, which interconnects more than 120 machines and runs at 3 megabits per second, show that a typical daily load for this system is about 1% of the system capacity. Peak loads (tending to occur at around noon, 4:00 PM, and 6:00 PM) tend to be less than 35% of capacity. Since appreciable delays occur only when the load approaches 100% of capacity, they do not seem likely to become a problem for most installations.

There are some other limitations on ETHERNET systems. First, individual cables should not be longer than 500 meters because the packet-retransmission-delay calculations must take into account the round-trip transmission time on the cable, which is a function of its length. Second, it is very important to have the transceiver-connectors exactly matched electrically to the cable. If there are mismatches then signal reflections can occur at the mismatch points, causing unacceptable contention problems. When such mismatches occur on a cable TV system, the viewer's eye-brain combination acts to ignore their unwanted effects, but computers are not so flexible.

A third limitation may be the user's wallet. ETHERNET is a sophisticated system, designed to handle large loads in highly automated office and laboratory environments. Typical costs of an ETHERNET installation in 1982 were about $6000 per node, with 1983 prices approaching $1,000.

OTHER LOCAL NETWORKS

For situations with more modest requirements, more modest (and less expensive) systems may do as well. The following are some of the possibilities available in 1982.

C-NET. Cromemco, Inc., has a local network system called C-NET. The C-NET system is another CSMA-CD system. Its design emphasis is on combining reliability of operation with a moderate (compared to some of the others) cost of about $1000 per node. Cromemco does this by using standard, high-reliability components throughout. The system uses a nominal data transmission rate of 500 kbits per second, but the rate can be varied from audio rates to 880 kbps. The idea behind the variable rate is that the system can be tailored to the needs of its users: a high-speed microcomputer-only network might use the 880 kbps rate; a system using a cable television as the distribution method might lean toward audio transmission rates, or whatever else might be appropriate for the circumstances. The system will accommodate up to 255 nodes per cable segment and, like ETHERNET, allows interconnected segments.

The normal cable for C-NET is a shielded twisted pair meeting military standard performance requirements and costing about one-tenth that of ETH-ERNET cable. Unlike some of the other systems, the C-NET cable interface is transformer-isolated from the cable to provide enhanced noise rejection (such as from lightning or motors in an industrial setting) and immunity of the network from failure of a node. The maximum allowable separation of stations on the cable is 2 km. The interface circuits were also designed to incorporate audio and video signals in the same cable, preparing the way for the ultimate multimedia local network.

OMNINET. OMNINET is a CSMA system, without collision detection, introduced in mid-1981 by Corvus Systems, Inc. of San Jose, California. Like ETHERNET's controller, the OMNINET system has a device called a trans-porter, containing its own 8-bit microprocessor, that performs similar functions. OMNINET will handle a data rate of 1 megabit per second and up to 64 stations. One of the stations is likely to be a hard-disk drive and controller that acts as a database resource for the network. The "cable" required for OMNINET is a simple shielded twisted pair. Corvus also manufactures a "gateway" for inter-connecting OMNINET to ETHERNET and other networks.

CLUSTER/ONE. NESTAR System, Inc., of Palo Alto, California, manufactures a system called Cluster/One that is designed to act as a resource-sharing system for popular mid-range personal computers such as the Apple II®, Commodore™, or Radio Shack computers. The data transfer rate for Cluster/One is roughly 80 kilobits per second. Cluster/One is not a CSMA system. It employs a network controller, called the Queen, that polls the "Drone" stations on the network for requests. The Queen circuitry is included as a package with a hard disk that is used as the central data resource of the system, containing a central file of applications programs as well as other data. The system is intended primarily for use in educational applications, although it should be appropriate for other applications requiring similar resource sharing. The Queen can handle two parallel 25-wire buses, each with up to 15 Drones attached. The Drones have their own controller circuits and ROM software to handle the interface protocols. Cluster/One includes a hard-disk operating system to handle disk access and interstation communications. The latter can include communications, via a modem, with other systems. Otherwise, the system is not compatible with the other systems described above.

An improved version of Cluster/One, called Cluster/One Model A, does use CSMA, without ETHERNET's direct collision detection scheme. Collisions are detected indirectly, via error appearances in the packet checksum.

CP/NET AND MP/NET. Digital Research Corporation, of Pacific Grove, California, produces two disk operating systems for microcomputer networks. These are not local networking systems in and of themselves. The systems allow resource sharing among the interconnected computers and provide a facility for electronic mail.

The difference between CP/NET and the local networking schemes described previously is that CP/NET is not tied to a specific network hardware configuration. This is accomplished by placing all the hardware-independent software in a separate I/O module that is accessible to the hardware-dependent portions of the system.

CP/NET operates in a network master/slave configuration. The "master" microcomputer has access to those resources, such as hard disks with central files, a system printer, a plotter, etc., that are considered "public" to the other users of the network. This microcomputer must also have the Digital Research MP/M™ multiprocessor operating system. The slave computers must be running Digital Research's CP/M™ operating system. This limits the use of CP/NET to those computers with 8080 or Z80 type processors and those that have a translator between the 8080 instruction set and their own instruction set (for instance, the Apple II). Each of the slave computers has access to its own private resources as well as to those of the master.

CP/NET uses a message packet consisting of a message format code, destination and source processor identifications, a CP/M function code, a data field size byte, and the actual message of arbitrary length. The system does not include either carrier-sensing or collision-detection provisions, leaving error detection to the user's discretion. That is, the purchaser of the CP/NET code must add his or her own error-detection software to the system. As with CP/M, Digital Research provides ample, if opaque, documentation to guide the system twiddler in this task.

MP/NET is similar to CP/NET except that there is no distinction between master and slave.

OTHER POSSIBILITIES FOR LOCAL NETWORKING

Some manufacturers provide much of the general-purpose hardware suitable for microcomputer networks without actually requiring that the communicator go the last step. For example, Cromemco has a sophisticated set of I/O processing boards for S-100 bus computers. These boards include "IOP" (Input/Output Processor) that, when combined with one or more "Quadart" boards (QUADruple UARTs), can support a substantial variety of intercomputer communications without bothering the main microprocessor of the computer. Each IOP has its own Z80 microprocessor, and space for 16 K bytes of RAM and up to 32 K bytes of ROM. The system has its own data bus, called the "C-Bus" by Cromemco, that allows communications among the IOP and up to 8 Quadarts, for a total of 32 devices per IOP. Cromemco's CDOS and CROMIX operating systems can handle up to 4 IOPs so that the hardware is capable of communicating with up to 128 slave devices per computer. Of course, the IOPs can be coupled with C-NET (or some other local network) to create networks within networks.

If anything, the rate of development of local and other computer networking methods, and of methods for combining computer-based and other forms of telecommunications, should increase in the 1980s. It is impossible in a printed book, with all the delays between my writing it and your buying it, to keep up-to-the-minute on the latest developments. Local networking is one of the most crowded and fastest lanes in the race to the automated office, so the situation is likely to change weekly for some time to come. However, the samples just given should give you an idea of the emerging possibilities.

10

ow that we have amassed this collection of facts on the processes of microcomputer telecommunications, it is time that we examine some of the applications of the technology. To what practical uses can it be put? This chapter considers a sampling of applications, together with the technological requirements for them, in the areas of gainful employment, entertainment, education, and security. Present realities as well as future possibilities are considered in this discussion.

NETWORK PROVIDERS

Although we have covered the concepts of telecommunication networks, and have explored some of the details of one (the telephone system) in previous chapters, we have spent little time on the emerging role of network providers and network information services. Many of the new services now being offered, or soon to be offered, depend upon computer communications. Like the telephone, they will eventually be available nationally, even globally. At present, some are available, at their lowest rates, only in major cities.

There are (at least) two levels of information-service provision. At the first level are what are called "value-added networks" (VANs) and "specialized common carriers." The VANs lease the actual transmission lines from other corporations, such as the telephone companies or the specialized common carriers, but add some special service to make the communications process more efficient or easier to use. Examples of VANs are TYMNET and GTE's TELENET. Both provide data transmission services using packet switching. They also provide interface hardware and software to make different types of data terminals or computers compatible with each other's for data transmission.

Specialized common carriers offer their own long-distance transmission lines to their customers. As a consequence, they compete directly with AT&T's Long Lines Division. MCI Telecommunications Corp. and Southern Pacific Communications Co. are two of the early entries in this field. SBS (Satellite Business Services), a creation of IBM, Aetna and ComSat General, is a solely-satellite specialized common carrier. The 1982 divestiture of AT&T from its local operating companies is certain to bring increased competition in this area. The likely result is that both AT&T and the specialized carriers will bring advanced data communications services to the market sooner than might otherwise have happened.

The next layer of network-service providers consists of firms offering various

Getting into Action

types of information through some form of telecommunication network. They provide information, not telecommunications. The most familiar service providers are the radio and TV broadcast companies. In the data-processing field there are numerous firms that provide computing services over telecommunications lines. Over the past twenty years this form of network information service has become a major industry. Two new information-service providers are becoming much more familiar to owners of personal computers. They are Source Telecommunications and CompuServe. These organizations take advantage of the fact that most business uses of network information services occur during working hours. After these hours the demand on their computers is significantly lessened. This leaves the companies with underused computers for which it would be nice to have a market. By making the computers available—at lower rates—to hobbyists and others who wish to use these more powerful machines for business, entertainment, or educational purposes, the companies thought to help spread the expense of the computers. In fact, the rate of growth of these services has been dramatic. CompuServe reported a 300% growth rate in 1981.

There are two categories of service provided by these higher-level network firms. The traditional service available from many of the firms is computation. The concept at the beginning of this field was that the large computer firms, or firms with large computers, could share the costs of their resources by renting them to smaller business customers. The service eventually expanded to the point where firms were organized specifically to provide these computing services, adding extra software and specialized applications programs as the market grew.

Other firms and some of the computer service firms then began to provide another kind of service, "databases." A database is simply a collection of information in a computer, arranged by means of various indexing procedures so that it is readily accessible: an electronic library complete with reference librarian. The database service provides the information itself, not the manipulation of it. The database service industry is growing rapidly. In the mid-1960s there were only a few databases stored on computers. By 1982 there were more than 1000 commercial computer-based databases in the United States, according to an expert at the USC NASA Industrial Applications Center. These range from highly specialized services, providing information only to regular subscribers, to publicly available systems such as the *New York Times* Index and the Dow Jones Information Service. Companies like CompuServe and The Source provide both computing and database services.

One other term that will be increasingly heard among users of some forms of databases is "videotex." A videotex system consists of a central computer (or network of computers) containing one or more databases, the telephone network (or equivalent), and a number of smart terminals that can decode signals from the computer (see Figure 10-1). A videotex terminal need not be a microcomputer, but a microcomputer can easily be used as a videotex terminal by adding software to emulate the videotex protocols, if the terminal can also display the videotex graphics characters. By 1990 videotex database systems are likely to be widespread in the United States, as much so as in Europe where they were first introduced.

In order to see how all this might affect your own world in the near future let us examine some of the possibilities.

MAKING IT ALL WORK

For many new technologies, the products of technological growth appeared first in offices and factories, where the expense of the new product could be rationalized in terms of its benefits to productivity. The same tends to be true of telecommunicating microcomputers. The more elaborate and sophisticated systems normally appear first in business situations. Later, as the price comes down and the system becomes easier to use, increasing numbers show up in homes. This clearly has been the situation in the early years of development of the microcomputer market. Here are some examples.

The Office

Microcomputers are finding their way into many offices as information workers begin to reap the benefits of automation. Most first-time applications of microcomputers in offices are in the stand-alone mode, for business analyses and text processing, but the advantages of telecommunication soon become evident in many office situations. Here it is the type of business need that determines the sort of telecommunication hardware and software that is needed. Needs can be broken into three general categories, depending on the telecommunications traffic involved.

LOW-USAGE TELECOMMUNICATIONS. This is the situation where the most appropriate hardware for telecommunications is a simple microcomputer-modem-telephone line combination. I suspect that this would take care of at least four-fifths of all inter- or intra-office computer telecommunications situations in the early to mid-1980s. Here are the key indicators of a low-usage situation.

- Textual communications between workers are infrequent. That is, Bill deals mainly with accounting problems, Sue with financial estimating, Phil with technical writing, Yoshio with product design, and each has an individual software package tailored for that person's job and microcomputer.

- Most information-processing tasks are small. Although "small" is getting larger every year in the micro world, the point here is that the job only occasionally requires that a bigger computer get involved in the information-processing task. The fact that a larger machine does need to be used every now and then indicates that some telecommunication capacity is required.

- Telecommunication, when needed, need not be at high speed—that is, a 300-baud transmission over the telephone would probably be adequate for all telecommunications needs; at most, an investment in a 1200-baud line might be worthwhile. A good example of this situation is the use of microcomputer-based text-processing software instead of a large, sophisticated package on a big computer somewhere, the latter requiring telecommunication. In many cases, even where final reduction to a photo-typeset master by the big machine is necessary, it is likely to be more effective to do all the draft preparation on a local microcomputer. When all this highly interactive work is done then, and only then, is the almost-final text sent to the big machine, so the penalty for slow telecommunication is incurred only once.

The analysis behind all this is the standard one of cost effectiveness. The least expensive way of telecommunicating with microcomputers is with a simple modem and a telephone line. In 1982, between $100 and $400 will buy telecommunication capability at rates up to 300 baud, including software. For higher rates, such as 1200 baud, the price hovers closer to $700 per microcomputer. The benefit exceeds the cost when the value of the time saved by the worker telecommunicating exceeds the expense of the telecommunications system. For many types of information work the break-even point can be reached in a few months, or less.

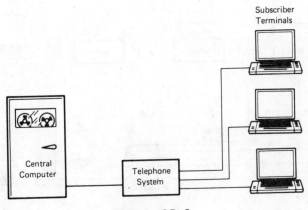

Figure 10-1
Videotex

On the other hand, if the information worker is spending a significant amount of time just trying to get on the system rather than accomplishing useful tasks, then the next steps in telecommunication sophistication are worth examining.

MODERATE USAGE SITUATIONS. The next step in complicating the telecommunication process comes when there is likely to be a more frequent need for inter-worker communication or for communication with other computing resources. This intermediate step involves the use of microcomputer-based multi-user systems. Here are the key indicators of this situation.

● Several workers need to share the same database, such as inventory, order files, client lists, or parts descriptions.

● Several workers use the same computer language and/or applications programs, and the cost of a multi-user software package is less than that of individual packages for each worker.

● There are high-cost resources, such as a letter-quality printer, that are used only occasionally by any single worker but must be available to all.

● Fairly high data-transmission rates must be achieved by some of the users some of the time.

In the simplest case, telecommunication as we have been discussing it in this book may not even be necessary. A simple setup that involves a single computer connected to a few (typically seven or fewer) terminals and run by a multi-user operating system (such as MP/M™, OASIS™, or one of the systems based on UNIX™) might be sufficient. Here the primary limitation may be the

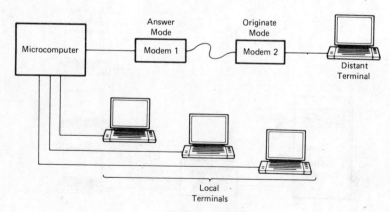

Figure 10-2
Multi-user Computer System with a Distant User

length of the cables between system users. If cable losses are severe, as could be the case if the lines were a few hundred feet in length, then a serial interface with a current-loop signaling system might do the trick. Failing that, the next level of escalation would be a pair of modems for each distant user; one at the microcomputer and one at the user's terminal, as illustrated in Figure 10-2.

If a relatively large database or a large number of applications programs must be shared by more than a few information workers, then it seems probable that one of the small local networking systems such as C-NET, OMNINET℠, or Cluster/One℠ may be advisable. Cost-benefit considerations are similar to the low-usage case. The telecommunication adapters for each participating microcomputer or "server" (such as the aforementioned letter-quality printer) have prices somewhat higher than those of simple modems, because they are not as simple as simple modems. On the other hand, several microcomputers can share a large hard-disk drive or a quality printer, thereby driving the cost per computer below what would be possible if equivalent resources were incorporated into individual microcomputer systems. In short, although the network is expensive, there may be significant economies of scale.

OFFICE AUTOMATION. If the cases just covered are still too tame for the sophisticated information worker, then we can get into the combination of microcomputers, mainframes and minicomputers, specialized computational resources, and telecommunication that is generally known as "office automation." This is not to say that what we have been considering has not been automation of the office. Rather, the term "office automation" is usually reserved for the more complicated systems, such as a densely populated ETHERNET (or similar moderate-to-high data-rate local network), possibly with TV and audio communications as well, interconnecting all of these systems. In a typical office automation scheme the system offers such utilities as electronic mail, centralized databases, intercommunicating calendars (to minimize time wasted in setting up meetings), and the like.

Table 10-1 illustrates a sample situation in the not so distant future. The elaborateness of the personal microcomputer work station depends on the variety of tasks its user must perform (and perhaps also on the user's status in the organizational hierarchy). Both the physical configuration of the microcomputer—its shape, size, color, and hardware components—and the complement of software normally used with it are job-specific. Color displays are normal among middle- and upper-level decision-makers and professional staff; so are personal, specialized databases, with access restrictions. These will be required increasingly as both the complexity of decisions and the data analysis and presentation supporting them grow. Each of the microcomputer stations, at all levels of the organization, has a communications controller so that the individual can keep in touch with the life of the organization.

Communications is the key to the well-functioning organization. The more familiar people are with the activities of the organization, its goals, and its

Table 10-1
Elements of an Automated Office

User	Personal Work Station	Work Station Utilities	Shared Utilities
Boss	Color display (Projection) Integral videophone High-resolution graphics Dual control • Local keyboard • Repeater of assistant's console Mouse or light pen	Personal calendar Data analysis packages Database manipulation controls Text processing Communications controller Encrypter/ decrypter	Master calendar Electronic mail Bulletin board Computer conferencing Teleconferencing Corporate databases • Personal • Financial • Accounting • Inventory • Research • Archives Document processing
Boss's administrative assistant	Color display Integral videophone High-resolution graphics Mouse or light pen	Personal calendar Copy of boss's calendar Text processing Data analysis packages Communications controller	
Professional staff member	Color display High-resolution graphics Mouse or light pen	Personal calendar Working database Database manipulation Data analysis Graphics generation Text processing Communications controller	
Clerk/typist	Monochrome display Keyboard	Personal calendar Optical character reader Text processing Communications controller	

progress toward them, the more satisfied and productive they tend to be. Effective communication promotes such familiarity. Thus there are a number of shared information facilities in the automated office. Central to these are the electronic message systems: the master calendar, electronic mail, the electronic bulletin board, and the conferencing systems. You have probably already noticed that *all* the telecommunication modalities are incorporated into the telecommunication systems in Table 10-1. Voice, video, and data are all assumed to be available on the network. To make this possible all are converted to digital form prior to transmission. These technologies are not widely available or inexpensive yet, but they should be in the last half of this decade.

The purpose of the master calendar is to keep a central file of the time commitments of the organization's staff. Note that the details of what a particular staff member is doing during a particular period of committed time are probably not kept by this database. What is important is that available time for meetings and conference is on file. This simple facility can drastically reduce the amount of time ordinarily wasted in attempts to set up meetings, particularly large ones. A typical scenario would go something like this:

> Debra walked into the office, sat down at her console, said in carefully modulated tones "Debra here," and inserted her ID card into the slot in the side of the console. The console responded, in equally rotund tones, "Good morning, Debra. Here is today's calendar." The display showed a list of prescheduled meetings covering most of the afternoon. The morning had three hours left open. Debra had been planning to use them for analyzing the service records for the past three months. The bottom line of the display, however, was flashing: *Raoul has requested a meeting at 11:30, subject: procedure modifications.* "I knew I should have listed that time as unavailable," thought Debra.

Electronic mail, the bulletin board, and computer conferencing are all variants on our central theme of transmission of messages from one computer to another. All of these variations require that some computer in the system act as a post office and/or broadcast station. Further, they require that the postbox computer be operating at any time the system is operating. In a typical electronic-mail system the postbox computer has a software package that is available to all users of the system. This package consists of routines for formatting the message, determining the name and address of the intended recipient and of the sender, and storing the message temporarily prior to forwarding. Figure 10-3 shows a typical message-transmission format. At the first opportunity, usually the next time the recipient logs in to the system, the postbox computer notifies the intended recipient that new mail is waiting. It may then send it and erase its own copy of the message or keep a copy until instructed otherwise.

Many electronic-mail systems have a number of other utilities as well. For example, the sender can have a series of different lists of recipients on file with the postbox computer. By identifying a particular list the sender can send the same message to everyone on the list, with but a single keystroke. To answer a message, the recipient merely enters an 'answer' command, usually a single keystroke, then keys in the reply. The postbox computer takes care of the "administrivia" of attaching all the proper addresses. Entire messages can be reviewed, or only the subject headings; separate files can be built of messages on a particular topic, or during a particular period of time, or from a specific sender; the files can be kept locally, or on the postbox computer.

"Computer conferencing" is a specialized form of electronic-message system in which all the messages between participants are supposed to have a common subject. The computer conference has the intriguing property of being able to

```
USC-ECL Micro600 Port selector
Which system? ecla [This asks the user to select among the
                    computers available on the 'host' system]
Connected

 USC-ECL System A, TOPS-20 Monitor 4(3263)-2
 There are 8+17 jobs and the Load Average is  1.09
@nilles testjob. [This is the log on procedure]
 Job 25 on TTY61 4-Dec-82 14:49:07
 Previous LOGIN: 26-Nov-82 11:24:15
 End of LOGIN.CMD.5
 You have mail from DUTTON at 1-Dec-82 12:47:10
@msg [This invokes the electronic mail system]
    MSG -- version of 11 August 1982
    Type ? for help, ? # for news
-+ 58   1 Dec  DUTTON at USC-ECL     Conferences (2051 chrs)
    Last read: 26-Nov-82 11:27:41; 57 old msgs, 58 msgs, 22 disk pages.
<- type recent messages
(msg. # 58, 2051 chars)
Date:  1 Dec 1982 1247-PST
From: DUTTON at USC-ECL
Subject: Conferences
To:   csteinfield at USC-ECL, estefferud at ECL, gasser at ECL,
To:   lievrouw at USC-ECL, nicol at USC-ECL, nilles at USC-ECL,
To:   seastman at ECLB, svenning at USC-ECL, rice at USC-ECL

              COMPUTER CONFERENCING ON ECLA

     There are now three computer conferences open to anyone  who
would  like  to  participate on ECLA.  These  conferences  were
established  as part of a course about computers as communication
media  offered  at  USC's  Annenberg  School  of  Communications.
Students  in  the course designed the conferences and will use them
to help study affects of computer mediated communication.  Please
feel free to participate in each of conferences.   One involves a
discussion  of video games and their likely social  and  economic
consequences.   A  second  conference  attempts to  arrive  at  a
definition of computer literacy, while the third elicits opinions
regarding  people's  preferences for a variety of  attributes  in
their [hypothetical] dating partners.
     The  Confer  computer  conferencing  program  is  used.   It
contains an extensive set of online help instructions.  We  have
also  created  a  small  help file for confer  available  at  the
executive  level.   To join any of the conferences,  simply  type
"confer<return>" when at the executive level.   To read the  help
file  before entering confer,  simply type "help confer" when the
executive  level.   These conferences are open to all who wish to
participate,  provided  they have an account on ECLA.   Please
inform  your friends and colleagues and enjoy the conferences!
--------
<- quit [Confirm]
    Good-bye.
```

Figure 10-3
An Electronic Mail Sample

continue over great lengths of time: days, weeks, even months. The conferrers can be all the members of the conference network, or just subgroups. Individuals can make statements to all the participants of the conference, to certain groups (as in the special distribution lists of electronic mail), or only to individual participants (this is known as "whispering"). In some conferencing systems individual comments in the conference cannot be altered once they are submitted. In other systems the author is free to edit prior comments to develop a final statement. It is possible for members of the conference to comment on the remarks made by others; these comments may be appended to the original remarks in the final conference record. In short, essentially all the formal and informal communication events that go on in a face-to-face conference can also occur in a computer conference, and there is one important new possibility: *it is not necessary for any two of the conferees to be "present" on the system at the same time in order for the conference to continue.* Thus, computer conferencing is clearly a critical liberation for harried knowledge workers who, in spite of the improvements afforded by a master calendar, cannot seem to meet at the same time.

"Teleconferencing" is at present not a technique involving microcomputers. The term refers to conferences that use the telephone or television, or some in-between method like slow-scan television, as the communications medium. In the next few years, though, these modes will become integrated with the microcomputer as their signals become digitized. Thus, in Table 10-1, the assumption is made that the boss's display console is equally capable of presenting high-quality sound and TV information, computer graphics, and alphanumeric information. All of this will be transmitted along the common network.

Telecommuting

Many of the office automation possibilities mentioned before are attainable with the "old standby" network, the telephone system. High-capacity data networks are desirable in the more exotic cases of combined data, voice, and color video, but they are not absolutely necessary for most of us. The reason that this is important is that the telephone system is so extensive. There are few places in the U.S. where there is no telephone service. Consequently, there are few places in the U.S. where an information worker could not set up a microcomputer and that realization raises the possibility of telecommuting.

"Telecommuting" is a term for the substitution of computers and communications for the daily commute to work. All the necessary technological steps have already been described for developing a telecommuting capacity with a microcomputer and a modem. Whether this is a good idea for an individual information worker depends on the particular job situation.

Telecommuting takes two primary forms. The form most people immediately think of when they first hear about telecommuting is working at home (as I am doing while writing this on my microcomputer). In this mode the telecommuter simply goes to some spot in the home—the den, a spare room, the living room—

turns on the microcomputer (or simply a terminal) and modem, logs in to the company computer, and begins the work day. Of course, for much information work it is not even necessary to be connected to the company computer except for brief periods of message or data transfer. A secretarial worker can take dictation via a telephone-answering device, convert it to text on the microcomputer, and then transmit the dataset to the company, all from a home office.

Home telecommuting is particularly appropriate for two classes of people: those who are constrained to stay at home, and those whose information jobs do not involve much face-to-face contact with others. The first class includes those whose mobility is impaired, such as the physically handicapped and parents of small children. The second includes writers; computer programmers; some consultants, scientists, engineers, and other professional people; those in the mail-order business (electronic or otherwise); and some secretarial workers and data-entry clerks. There were probably a few thousand such telecommuters in 1982.

The other form of telecommuting involves regional/local work centers. A telecommuter could work at the company center nearest to home, the local center, rather than at some central location requiring, in most large urban areas in the United States, an average commute of ten miles. The critical point in both forms of telecommuting is that *the work location of the information worker is independent of the job held.* The accounting department becomes a logical, rather than a physical, entity. It exists as a network of telecommunications-connected workers rather than as a collection of workers and desks all in the same room or on the same floor of a building. A company might have four or five local centers scattered around its headquarters city, located in areas close to where most of its employees live, with accountants (or designers, or engineers, or whatever) in all of them.

The reason for the likely dominance of the second mode of telecommuting is partly technological, but largely sociological. Technologically, a local network capable of transmitting information, in all the necessary formats, between the homes of individual workers will not be practical for decades. Yet it will be necessary for many information workers in the near future to have access to relatively sophisticated forms of communication, processing, and display, of the type made possible by local networks. This access will be readily achieved in local work centers interconnected by wideband data links.

Sociologically, people need to have face-to-face contact with others at some time during the course of their work. We are social animals. Much of the training in the skills and attitudes of worklife is best achieved in interpersonal situations. A substantial part of corporate life involves the informal communications that occur then. Similarly, distractions in the home can impede effective work there. Managers also seem to feel more comfortable when they can see the employees for whom they have responsibility. For all these reasons, and many others, it is likely that most telecommuters will work in this sort of environment.

The Information Entrepreneur

The rapid increase in the capabilities of information technologies seems to be producing an equally rapid increase in demand for specialized kinds of information. This demand produces a natural climate for the rise of all sorts of information entrepreneurs. One group has been growing for several years: the independent computer programmer. We can expect that, as more computers become telecommunication-equipped, the number and diversity of these entrepreneurs will increase. Many will start as part-timers, working as telecommuters during evening or weekend hours. They will sell their services through the traditional methods: friends in the business, ads in trade magazines, etc. They will also begin to sell them through the specialized information brokerage, in itself a new form of entrepreneurialism, and through local or national network information services. For most of the applications noted here, the budding entrepreneur does not need a massive hardware investment to begin operations. A microcomputer capable of handling the information to be transferred and having a telecommunication capability is all that is required.

PLAYING AROUND

Telecommunicating microcomputers are not confined to serious business. The *real* reason most people buy microcomputers is because they are fascinating toys; they are even addictive. Of course, the reasons these same people *give* for buying their microcomputers are quite straight-laced and rational—but we know better.

Community Bulletin Boards

Any attempt to print an accurate count of the number of community bulletin boards in existence, given the delay of several months between the completion of this manuscript and the publishing of the book, would meet with certain disaster. There are hundreds, perhaps thousands. Some are as evanescent as mayflies, appearing and disappearing overnight. Others have been around since the very beginnings of microcomputer telecommunication, using software developed by Ward Christensen and Randy Suess of the Chicago Area Hobbyist Exchange and known as CBBS℠ for "Computerized Bulletin-Board System."

The bulletin board was mentioned earlier as a special case of an electronic-message system. It is what the title implies, a dial-up computer database that contains messages left by various and sundry callers. The requirements for operating a CBBS are a microcomputer, an answer/originate modem, and a package of software. The latter can be obtained from Randy Suess (whose address at the time this was written was 5219 Warwick, Chicago, IL 60641) for a nominal fee.[1] CBBSes come in various flavors. There are general-purpose bulletin boards,

---

[1]For more information, see Jim Mills, "ABBS, CBBS, FBBS, RBBS, Etc., Maybe You'd Like To Start One Too?" *Lifelines* 2, no. 5 (October 1981): 20–22.

and there are those specializing in topics such as astronomy and genealogy. The degree of specialization seems to be limited only by the imagination of the users.

Another system designed as a public electronic-mail service is PCNET (for Personal Computer NETwork). It is a much more complex system, based on a several-layer communication protocol patterned after ARPANET. It was designed primarily by people involved with such networks in their daily work. The idea behind the PCNET development is to have a communications system that is entirely hardware-independent; any computer equipped with PCNET software will be able to communicate with any other similarly equipped machine (an ability of CBBS, too). PCNET also has a software package called PAN, after the illegitimate son of Hermes, the Greek god. "HERMES" happens to be the name of a sophisticated electronic mail system developed by Bolt, Beranek and Newman, Inc. for large minicomputers. Unlike CBBS, which is an ordinary asynchronous serial-data communications system, PCNET uses a form of packet switching. Members of the PCNET group are experimenting with packet-switched CB radio. At the time this was written, the address of the PCNET project was c/o People's Computer Company, 1263 E. Camino Real, Box E, Menlo Park, California 94025.[2]

Interactive Games

Conversing via a bulletin board is a little like slow-motion ham radio. It takes a long time to type long messages. For more excitement in your life, look for multiplayer interactive video games. The idea is that a normal, placid livid-color-and-sound personal-computer video game will be even further enhanced by allowing several players to participate, each with an individual display of the action. The task of the telecommunication link between the players is to coordinate the data and displays so that all are given an accurate picture of the current status of the game, or at least as much as they ought to know of it.

This task is not trivial, even if all the players are using the same type of hardware. Display-hardware compatibility is particularly important. Without it, the additional burden of translating between differing display methods will make the job much more difficult for the interfacing software. The job is not that easy for the telephone system, either. For two players it is a relatively simple matter. The two establish a connection via their modems and blaze away. For more than two players one or more must be able to communicate with two other players in an open-loop network, as shown in Figure 10-4. Here players B and C must either have two telephone lines and two modems each, or must have a rapid dial-redial system to relay data between the players.

In the first case A telephones B's first number, B relays the information via his second number to C's first number, and so on. Since all connections are

---

[2]For more information on PCNET, see Dave Caulkins, "The Personal Computer Network [PCNET] Project: A Progress Report," *Dr. Dobb's Journal of Computer Calisthenics and Orthodontia* 5, no. 6 (June/July 1980): 10–14.

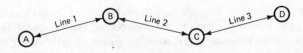

**Figure 10-4
A Multi-player Game Network Using the Telephone
System**

made all the time, this version is the fastest-paced (and most expensive in hardware). In the second case A dials B, sends a message and receives a confirmation and, possibly, a return message and hangs up. B then dials C and repeats the A–B process, and so on. Clearly, with many players this would get tedious at best.

With packet CB radio, however, we may have some interesting possibilities. The situation is topologically identical to a bus structure, with the radio channel serving as the bus. Transmissions between players would be in brief packets (the contention issues were discussed in Chapter 9). If the game were to occur over some of the lower of the frequencies used by amateur radio operators, without the line-of-sight limitations of CB, the game could become truly international. And with a communication satellite in the chain . . . . . .

THE LOCATIONLESS SCHOOL

Microcomputer communication need not be restricted to work and play. One particularly rewarding use of microcomputers is for education. As in the case of all the examples given earlier, the addition of telecommunication capability to the microcomputer makes it accessible to, and by, any computer-based source of information. One important future source is the school.

Telecommuting to School

Computer-based instruction, when well executed, has two very significant attributes that distinguish it from most other forms of education. First, it is intensely personal: tailored closely to your learning patterns, and enabling you to learn at your own pace. Second, if it can be used with your personal computer, it is time-independent. These two features give this form of instruction a degree of flexibility that cannot be matched in the ordinary classroom situation. It is only fair to point out that the reverse is also true: the ordinary classroom situation can provide learning experiences that are unmatchable in computer-based instruction. But those who are pressed for time, or have none available that matches the usual academic schedule, and those who are interested in developing certain fact-based skills, may find education via computer telecommunications very suitable.

The computer doesn't care about your age, height, color, sex, religion, shape, intelligence, or preferences in friends. If you are too young to go to school, the computer may help you learn to read and write (type). You can't be too old to go to school; you can't be too immobilized to go to school. Over the next decade, as the information revolution progresses, a great variety of computer-based educational software will become available, covering almost any subject. Much of it will be available via telecommunication.

The Electronic University

In the United States the universities were the first users of telecommunication as a vital link in teaching those who were unable to attend school during regular hours. Remote education services started, naturally enough, with various forms of telephone conferencing. Teachers would arrange conference calls with their students at home or in offices, and the class would go on. In some state university systems, different campuses were interconnected so that particular courses could be shared among all the interested students in the university system.

In the late '60s Stanford University added TV to the array of technologies fully available for instructional purposes—not that TV had not been used for educational purposes before then; the difference was that the Stanford system, like the telephone systems, was interactive. Since then a number of universities in the U.S. have developed interactive instructional TV systems (or IITVs) with great success. The University of Southern California, for example, has a system that includes 29 remote sites that can receive instructional programs. At each of these students can use a return audio line to ask questions of, or make comments to, the instructor (or the program monitor if the main program is videotaped). Most of the remote stations are located in the offices of major corporations in the area. Most of the courses deal with engineering or business topics. Employees of the corporations can study at their job locations; they need not commute long distances (20 miles or more in several cases) to the main campus. In fact, many students earn advanced degrees entirely with the IITV system.

IITV systems are expensive. They do not use the commercial broadcast TV frequencies, but higher frequencies, which require more sophisticated receiving equipment. Hence there is little chance that the average individual could afford to have an IITV receiver at home for the purpose of getting a university education. Enter the microcomputer.

Within the next few years, the wedding of microcomputers and educational TV will be consumated. In 1982, most educational TV systems were strictly analog: replicas, although interactive ones, of broadcast TV. But experiments with adding computer-based instructional methods were already in full swing. Several forms of interactive instruction are possible and will be economically feasible. Here are some of them.

"STANDARD" COMPUTER-AIDED INSTRUCTION. The school sends instructional software to the student's computer via the telephone system, cable TV networks, or regular mail (on tape cassettes or floppy disks). The student's answers to the questions and exercises in the software, and other data on the student's progress, are sent by telephone to the central computer on the main campus. The instructor can keep track of progress, keep grades, suggest supplementary materials, and so forth, just as in a face-to-face course, except that the link with the student is via electronic mail. The student needs only a personal computer; a modem suitable for the communication system, telephone or cable; and the necessary textbooks, if any, in order to take the course at the time, place, and pace of his choosing.

COMPUTER VIDEO. Frequently it is not enough to have simple text displays of everything. Some instructional material demands the use of pictures or complex graphics. Because of the proliferation of types of graphic displays in the computer market—that is to say, the lack of uniform standards for graphic display—it is economically unattractive for a producer of educational software to include pictorial routines for all likely receiving computers. One way around this stumbling-block is to use graphic presentations only where there are some standards, where the software producer has some hope of "portability" of the educational product. This path involves the use of commercial videotape or videodisc recording. In this process the textual material, in digital form, is somehow combined with the pictorial material (the techniques differ), and so the composite material presented to the student is much richer than the bare text captured by the computer.

In a typical situation of this sort the school giving a course might transmit the pictorial material to the students via a cable-TV system; they would tape it on their video recorders. The transmission could be done in the middle of the night, when there would be no conflicts for recording time. A student ready to take a lesson would dial up the instructional system computer and get the software via the telecommunication link—or the computer software might be embedded in the original video material. The advantage of having it separate is that the system can then have instructional responses specially tailored for each student. As student X dials up the computer system it, or the human instructor, can send an augmented (or accelerated, if the student is a fast learner) set of software for the lesson in question. In this way the ability to maintain dynamic progress in the software is maintained while the more expensive part of the production, the video material, stays constant.

Although video tape is the most likely near-term means for storage of such instructional materials, video disks will probably predominate in the long term, mainly for one reason: the video disk is a random access device like a floppy disk. Thus it is easy to arrange a course in a series of linear modules but have them randomly accessible, or reaccessible, in accordance with the student's progress through the course ("programmed instruction"). Video tapes are linear media. It is necessary to go past all intervening material if one is to get from one module to another. This inability to jump is not a disastrous complication; it simply means that a system based on video tape involves more "dead" time than would one based on video disk.

For all of these forms of education, the critical factor is the ability of the computer to allow the tailoring of the material presented, according to the student's abilities and available time. There is no other practical way to bring education to many people, particularly to adults who can not take the time for education in the traditional system. The telecommunicating microcomputer can bring this new freedom of "informability" to many who could not otherwise hope to have it. It may thus even be the technology which solves the problems created by the inability of most people today to understand and control the world which so many other modern technologies have shaped.

BIBLIOGRAPHY

The following is a collection of books and articles for those who may be interested in further reading on the topic of microcomputer telecommunications and networks.

Bemer, R. W. "Inside ASCII, Part I." *Interface Age* (Cerritos, Calif.) 3, no. 5 (May 1978): 96–102.

————. "Inside ASCII, Part II." *Interface Age* (Cerritos, Calif.) 3, no. 6 (June 1978): 64–74.

Caulkins, Dave. "The Personal Computer Network (PCNET) Project." *Dr. Dobb's Journal* 5, no. 6 (June 1980): 10–15.

Caulkins, Dave, and David C. Harris. "PAN: One Activity of the PCNET Project." *Dr. Dobb's Journal* 6, no. 2 (February 1981): 17, 37.

Crane, Ronald C., and Edward A. Taft. "Practical Considerations in Ethernet Local Network Design." Palo Alto, Calif.: Xerox Corporation, 1980.

Cravis, Howard. "Local Networks for the 1980s." *Datamation* 27, no. 3 (March 1981): 98–104.

Down, P. J., and F. E. Taylor. *Why Distributed Computing?* Manchester, England: NCC Publications, 1976.

Electronic Industries Association (EIA). "Application Notes for EIA Standard RS-232-C," Industrial Electronics Bulletin No. 9. Washington, D.C.: EIA Engineering Department, 1971.

————. *EIA Standard RS-232-C.* Washington, D.C.: EIA Engineering Department, 1969.

————. *EIA Standard RS-366-A.* Washington, D.C.: EIA Engineering Department, 1979.

Fisher, Eugene, and C. W. Jensen. *PET and the IEEE 488 Bus (GPIB).* Berkeley, Calif.: Osborne/McGraw-Hill, 1981.

Gilette, Dean. "Telematics: The Integration of Computing and Telecommunications." *ComputerWorld* 15, no. 11 (18 March 1981): 33–38.

Glossbrenner, Alfred. *The Complete Handbook of Personal Computer Communications.* New York, N.Y.: St. Martin's Press, 1983.

Goldberger, Alex. "A Designer's Review of Data Communications." *Computer Design* 20, no. 5 (May 1981): 103–112.

Green, P. E., Jr. "An Introduction to Network Architectures and Protocols." *IEEE Transactions on Communications,* vol. COM-284 (April 1980): 413–424.

Handler, Gary; Steven Katz; and Steven Markman. "Managing Private Electronic Networks." *Bell Laboratories Record* 57, no. 11 (December 1979): 320–324.

Hellman, Martin E. "The Mathematics of Public Key Cryptography." *Scientific American* 241, no. 2 (August 1979): 146–157.

Hiltz, Starr Roxanne, and Murray Turoff. *The Network Nation: Human Communication via Computer.* Reading, Mass.: Addison-Wesley, 1978.

Jurenko, John A. *All About Modems.* Huntsville, Ala.: Universal Data Systems, 1981.

Kleiner, Art. "A Survey of Computer Networks." *Dr. Dobb's Journal* 5, no. 6 (June 1980): 6–9.

Martin, James. *Telecommunications and the Computer,* 2d ed. Englewood Cliffs, N.J.: Prentice-Hall, 1976.

McNamara, John E. *Technical Aspects of Data Communication.* Bedford, Mass.: Digital Equipment Corp., 1977.

McQuillan, John M., and Vinton G. Cerf, eds. *A Practical View of Computer Communications Protocols.* Los Alamitos, Calif.: IEEE Computer Society, 1978.

Metcalfe, Robert M., and David R. Boggs. "Ethernet: Distributed Packet Switching for Local Computer Networks." *Communications of the ACM* 19, no. 7 (July 1976).

Nilles, Jack M. *Exploring the World of the Personal Computer.* Englewood Cliffs, N.J.: Prentice-Hall, 1982.

Nilles, Jack M.; F. Roy Carlson, Jr.; Paul Gray; and Gerhard J. Hanneman. *The Telecommunications-Transportation Tradeoff: Options for Tomorrow.* New York, N.Y.: John Wiley and Sons, 1976.

Power, Gerard L. "A Survey of Distributed Network Architectures." *ComputerWorld* 15, no. 11 (18 March 1981): 39–63.

Shoch, John F., and Jon A. Hupp. "Measured Performance of an Ethernet Local Network." Palo Alto, Calif.: Xerox Corporation, 1980.

Sirbu, Marvin A., Jr. "Automating Office Communications: The Policy Dilemmas." *Technology Review* (October 1978): 50–57.

Slana, M. F., and H. R. Lehman. "Data Communications Using the Telecommunication Network." *Computer* 14, no. 5 (May 1981): 73–88.

Toth, Frank. "Serial Communications and Interface Circuits in Microprocessor Systems." *Interface Age* (Cerritos, Calif.) 6, no. 4 (April 1981): 82–87.

Wingfield, Mike. "Build An Intercomputer Data Link." *Byte* 6, no. 4 (April 1981): 252–288.

———. *CP/NET Microcomputer Network Control Program: User's Guide.* Pacific Grove, Calif.: Digital Research, 1980.

———. *Data Communications: A User's Handbook.* Sunnyvale, Calif.: Racal-Vadic, 1981.

———. *The Ethernet—A Local Area Network: Data Link Layer and Physical Layer Specifications.* Stamford, Conn.: Xerox Corporation, 1980.

———. *Proceedings of the Computer Networking Symposium.* Los Alamitos, Calif.: IEEE Computer Society Press, 1980.

INDEX